A View from the Fog

A Story of Grief and Loss, and Faith and Hope

JADA D. L. HODGSON

WESTBOW
PRESS®
A DIVISION OF THOMAS NELSON
& ZONDERVAN

Scripture taken from the Holy Bible, NEW INTERNATIONAL VERSION®. Copyright © 1973, 1978, 1984, 2011 by Biblica, Inc. All rights reserved worldwide. Used by permission. NEW INTERNATIONAL VERSION® and NIV® are registered trademarks of Biblica, Inc. Use of either trademark for the offering of goods or services requires the prior written consent of Biblica US, Inc.

Scripture taken from the Contemporary English Version © 1991, 1992, 1995 by American Bible Society, Used by Permission.

This book is a work of non-fiction. Unless otherwise noted, the author and the publisher make no explicit guarantees as to the accuracy of the information contained in this book and in some cases, names of people and places have been altered to protect their privacy.

WestBow Press books may be ordered through booksellers or by contacting:

WestBow Press
A Division of Thomas Nelson & Zondervan
1663 Liberty Drive
Bloomington, IN 47403
www.westbowpress.com
1 (866) 928-1240

Because of the dynamic nature of the Internet, any web addresses or links contained in this book may have changed since publication and may no longer be valid. The views expressed in this work are solely those of the author and do not necessarily reflect the views of the publisher, and the publisher hereby disclaims any responsibility for them.

Any people depicted in stock imagery provided by Thinkstock are models, and such images are being used for illustrative purposes only. Certain stock imagery © Thinkstock.

ISBN: 978-1-5127-5592-3 (sc)
ISBN: 978-1-5127-5594-7 (hc)
ISBN: 978-1-5127-5593-0 (e)

Library of Congress Control Number: 2016915002

Print information available on the last page.

WestBow Press rev. date: 09/16/2016

Contents

Dedication

I have been incredibly blessed in the family God gave me. Years ago as I studied for the Bar Exam, my brother, Wayne Hodgson, came in saying, "I want some ice cream." Rather ungraciously, I invited him to go and get some. He did not want store bought but specialty ice cream. I did not have time to drive forty miles to the nearest Baskin-Robbins for ice cream, because I needed to study. He said Olathe was not what he had in mind. We ended up driving to the nearest Braum's eighty miles away in July in a pick-up truck air-conditioned only by three open windows loudly singing Aerosmith and Guns N' Roses. We spent the afternoon together, because Wayne had seen my level of exhaustion. He knew better than I did how much I needed a break. I love this man beyond all reason and understanding. He is my hero and my best friend. I will always be grateful that Wayne is my brother.

Dara and Layton Hodgson, my niece and nephew, are the lights of my life, as they were to my parents. It is so much fun to talk with and spend time with Dara and Layton. I want them to know that "I love you more…to infinity and beyond." I think I win this round!!

I love dolphins. When one dolphin in a pod is injured or ill, two healthy dolphins immediately come to help. They swim under the dolphin in trouble and support her. They bring the ailing dolphin to the surface so she can breathe. Dolphins help each other. These wonderful women are my pod; Jane Magathan, Lindsey Jaccard Walton, Juanita Bartel, Jamie Krone, and Dorothy Welch. A dolphin pod would never abandon one of its own, and these women have never left me.

I am grateful to Captain Mike Talcott and Detective Tim Brown of the Miami County Sheriff's Office. They were most gracious and kind when they came to tell me about the accident. I appreciate the compassion that they showed me that dreadful day.

Finally, I dedicate this work to the memory of my dear parents, Willis and Beth Hodgson. They taught me to pursue my dreams, never to settle, and that I am loved. They instilled in me the faith that has sustained me in their loss.

(Mom and Pop Galveston Ferry)

Foreword

by Juanita M. Bartel, MA, LPC, Retired
Board Certified Chaplain

In writing this Foreword for Jada's book my mind goes to the many sessions we experienced together in therapy. I remember the very first day she came to my office. She had two primary expectations; first to understand the grieving process and second to understand where she was in the process with planning for the next steps. Definitely lofty goals, because she was on a two month leave of absence from work and wanted to proceed at a "normal" rate of grief.

My response was that there is never a "normal" to grief. The first session was the beginning of recognizing that a "fog" had entered her existence. After reading Jada's manuscript and walking with her in her journey, I am so refreshed by her honesty in sharing her feelings and questions in her journey; the sense of a foreign feeling called "unsafe," the difficulty identifying herself with "who am I now," since Mom and Pop have died?

I remember sharing with Jada this quotation from Rainier Maria Rilke, "Be patient toward all that is unsolved in your hearts...try to love the questions themselves like locked rooms and like books that are written in a very foreign tongue. Do not now seek the answers, which cannot be given you because you would not be able to live them, and the point is, to live everything. Live the questions now. Perhaps you will then gradually, without noticing it, live along some distant day into the answer. (Rilke, M. R. 1903. *Letters to a young poet*, New York: W. W. Norton. M. S. Herter Norton, Trans., P. 27)" Little did I know then, that Jada was in the process of driving with a very heavy foot, wanting to "speed" her way to the finish line! There was to be NO "gradual" to this thing called grief!!

We grieve to the extent that we have loved!! She loved her parents and loves her family. Walking with Jada, and sometimes running with her, she has definitely wanted to push herself through the process—pushing through the fog has continued to keep her focused on slowing down and learning to care for herself in the process. Jada's integrity of grief is a gift to all of us with her willingness to prod through the fog.

I am honored that Jada asked me to write this foreword. The greatest joy I have in my life is to be a part of God's healing process in someone else's journey. We have journeyed together, learned together, laughed together, and even cried together. As you read the following words, remember that life has not ended; we continue to live without the physical presence of our loved ones, only to honor our losses by sharing our stories, realizing each day the impact that these ones that are gone have continued to have in our lives.

It Begins

The Fog Sets In

As thick fog developed, Dorothy and I decided to caravan home. As the more experienced driver, I would lead. There were lighter patches of fog along the way. I used those to speed up hoping to get home as soon as possible. When I sped up, though, Dorothy's headlights fell further behind. I slowed down each time so she could catch up. The fog thickened as the sun set. In the darkness, people passed who had no better visibility than we did. It was not always possible to see the road's center line. South of Garnett the highway split. Dorothy was to take one branch and I the other. I pulled over to see if she wanted company on the remainder of her trip. She went on by, okay to go on alone. We were in more familiar territory. When I got home, I called to be sure that she had arrived safely. We had made it home through the fog.

Coming home, I led Dorothy through the fog. On February 22, 2015, Dorothy began leading me through another kind of dense fog. My parents died in an automobile accident that afternoon. With that, my mind went away into the fog. Dorothy and other friends who knew the way, who had been in the fog themselves, began to lead me. My journey through grief's fog has been like that earlier trip. There have been people who breezed past me as though there was no fog. For them, the world had not been shockingly disrupted. They did not know. There have been patches where the fog has dissipated some, and I thought it was going to clear completely. It settles back in and dissipates again. I have been following people more experienced in navigating the fog of grief who know the territory intimately. They guide me, because they know where we are going.

I have lived this year in the fog of grief. My mind simply failed to work as it always had. I know from my reading that the fog is a common part of the process of grief. In the fog, I could not see my way from one task to another. I could not see a future without my parents. I could not see the need to go to my office or meet the needs of my clients.

In the fog, it is difficult to see your way. For those entering the fog of grief and loss, I offer my view from the fog. I hope that some of these insights will be helpful to you. I know that some will not be. If you are looking for answers, you will not find them here. I hope that you will find in these pages that you are not alone, and you are not "doing grief" wrong. All I have to offer is my experience within the fog and the hope that you, too, will move through it.

I am a Certified Lay Minister in the United Methodist Church.

I am an Elder Law Attorney.

I am an adult orphan.

I am still moving through the fog.

Beth Elaine Hodgson, aka "Mom," was a United Methodist pastor. She led the Plum Creek United Methodist Church for seventeen years. She was a room mother, a Scout leader, and an advocate for her kids. I love her dearly. I miss her terribly.

Willis Dean Hodgson, aka "Pop," was a retired public accountant. He was an active member of the Plum Creek United Methodist Church. He was my sports-watching buddy and my niece and nephew's super-fan. I love him dearly. I miss him terribly.

My family and my faith are inextricably intertwined. My parents enveloped me in faith from birth. We always attended worship and special celebrations together. Jesus has always been a member of my family and we of his. My family is foundational to an understanding of who I am. Mom could not go more than three days without talking with my brother and me on the phone. If she did not see her grandkids for three days, she became physically ill. She would have Pop drive by the school for a chance at a Dara or Layton sighting. My parents were my notary and witness in my law practice. Mom and I collaborated on sermon and worship ideas. We lived together, travelled together, ate together, and worshipped together. We were joined at the hip. This is the nature of my loss.

This is the story of life without my parents. It is my view from the fog. In the following pages you will find some transcripts of texts with one of my dearest friends and excerpts from a few of the sermons I have preached since the accident. You may find the transcripts of texts to be a bit clunky, but I want you to hear from Jane in her own words. She shared both wisdom and love. I kept a journal. Excerpts from it also appear. I pray that you will find peace in your journey through the fog.

The Knock at the Door

Sunday, February 22, 2015, began like a normal day, but that is not how it would end. Mom played the piano for church for me. Mom then preached at Plum Creek. I was to lead a Bible study that afternoon, so my parents met me for lunch. I left the restaurant before they did, saying, "I'll be home as soon as I can. I love you." I got home at about 3:00, and it seemed odd that they were not home. They should have been about an hour ahead of me. The next day was Wayne's birthday, so I assumed that they had stopped off to see him on the way. They were never very good about taking their cell phones with them. It was not surprising to be unable to reach them.

Pop had lost his garage door opener, so I was listening for a knock on the door asking me to let them in the garage. At about 4:30, there was a knock, but it was not Pop. Two officers from the Miami County Sheriff's Office stood at the door. I have almost no memory of the actual conversation. I do remember the officers' kindness and compassion. They asked if I knew Willis and Beth Hodgson. I said that I was their daughter. They showed me driver's license photos which I confirmed belonged to Mom and Pop. They came into the house and asked me to sit down with them. I did not sit down. Somehow, I could not sit down. Whatever I was about to hear, I had to take it on my feet. "There has been an accident. Your parents were killed at the scene." It took me the longest time to figure out what they were saying to me. Until they said the dreadful words "accident" and "killed at the scene," I had no idea why the officers were there. Even then, it took a moment to get it. There it was. In two sentences, my world changed forever. "There has been an accident. Your parents were killed at the scene." Finally, I managed to ask what had happened. They gave me some sanitized details including that the car had caught fire.

The officers had questions but first asked if there was someone I needed to call. I wanted to call Wayne, but I could not remember his number. Actually, I could barely figure out how to operate the phone in my hand. I had to look up Wayne's number on my cell phone. The fog had already begun to descend. I finally sat down to figure out how to use the phone. I called Wayne. He came immediately. We answered the officers' questions including providing a list of surgeries that might help them to identify the bodies. We were never asked to make a visual identification. There was apparently nothing visually identifiable left of Mom or Pop. We never saw my parents again. That inability to see Mom and Pop again has been difficult. There is this blank space where they should be.

After the officers left, Wayne and I decided who must be notified immediately. He agreed to tell our Uncle George, Mom's brother. Wayne then had to tell my niece and nephew that Grammie and Grampa were gone. I called the Princeton and Plum Creek United Methodist Churches asking for activation of the prayer chains there as a way to get the word out quickly. I had to call in a terrible favor. Years ago, Mom asked a dear friend, David Wilson from the Plum Creek church, to do her funeral. I desperately did not want to make that call. David graciously agreed. While Wayne and I scrambled to notify the people who needed to hear it directly from us, the accident was already being reported on the local news. Some of the people who should have received personal word from us probably got it from Channel 4 instead. I will always regret that. I can't change it, but I still regret it.

Sunday night or maybe Monday morning I grabbed a legal pad and started making a list of the things Wayne and I would have to do right away. I listed the phone calls to be made: the Church, special friends, insurance companies, and the funeral home. Another page contained candidates for pall bearers. There was a page for funeral notes. I jotted down Mom and Pop's birthdates and Social Security numbers so that they would be handy. Over the next weeks as I drew lines through various calls and activities completed, with notes for follow-up, the list became messy and hard to follow. I would copy the remaining tasks on a new page, adding others as we thought of them. Wayne and I split the initial list and worked on it together on Monday morning sitting in what had suddenly become my living room. **Making that list was a first step in moving through the fog.** I am someone who needs to have a plan. I needed that list as a lifeline. Over a year later, I still have that notebook.

By the time I posted the deaths on Facebook on Sunday night, a friend had posted a prayer request for my family. She had seen the report of the accident on the news. The response was immediate and overwhelming. There was so much love.

On Monday morning, I began to make notification calls. That is when I began to realize how many peoples' lives my parents had touched. Pop always preferred to do business face to face and with a hand shake. He drove thirty miles each month to pay the electric bill in person rather than stick a stamp on it. He always handled insurance questions face to face in our agent's office. He would talk with people he met about his family and theirs, making friends wherever he went. I knew that I needed to be as businesslike and matter of fact as possible in making these accident notification calls, so that I would be able to get through them. I was not thinking about the impact my calls would have on the people on the other end of the line. I called the insurance agent first. "My name is Jada Hodgson. I need to report a fatality accident. My parents, Willis and Beth, were killed in a single car accident yesterday afternoon. What information do I need to provide to begin the claim process?" There was a sharp intake of breath on the other end of the line. The agent said, "I am so sorry. I need just a minute. Did you say, Willis and Beth Hodgson were killed?" "Yes." "I am just shocked and terribly saddened. I just cannot believe that they are gone. They were always so nice when they came in..." When she could speak again, she offered her, obviously sincere, condolences and told me that she would begin processing the claim immediately. This sort of conversation was repeated numerous times over a year and a half. My folks were well and truly loved in their community.

On Tuesday, Jane and her mom brought supper from KFC. It is funny what becomes comfort food for us. Pop never liked KFC, because they always seemed to get his order wrong. KFC was a rarity in our house. It has become a staple in mine. A couple of months after the accident, I found myself on the way to Paola to KFC on a Tuesday night. I realized that I had made that same trek every Tuesday night since the accident. The love Jane and Sue showed me made KFC a part of my grieving ritual, comfort food, and important to me in ways I had never dreamed possible. It is funny how the ordinary becomes vitally important in times like this.

The three hour visitation was an ordeal. I am an introvert. I need to retreat to a solitary place to recover from shock or loss.

I was surrounded by 400 friends and colleagues of my parents all wanting to comfort me. All I wanted to do was escape, but there was to be no escape. There was no escaping any of this.

Because of the injuries my parents received, the autopsies took extra time. My parents died on Sunday, and the visitation was not until Thursday evening. This gave us time to make the arrangements in manageable segments. Most people make arrangements and have services within about three days. We had nearly a week. One day, we selected the caskets and flowers and handled service arrangements. One day, we selected music and burial plots and met with the preachers. Wayne and I have been partners in every decision. I never would have been able to do this without him. One evening, I selected and emailed photographs for the video display while Wayne prepared the music cd.

Since each detail was handled individually, each detail seemed manageable in itself. This led me to dread the visitation. That is when we would see the whole thing all together for the first time, caskets and flowers and finality. I have little recollection of the twenty-four hours period from the visitation through the funeral dinner. That is probably best. Some things I do remember.

I remember the long line of people who wanted to say that they had loved my parents. I remember Dara and Layton hovering between their dad and me, watching over us both. I remember a dear friend bringing me tea from Sonic. I remember sitting at the cemetery cuddled up with Layton wondering if we would ever feel warm again. I remember everyone's kindness. I remember Kaden's milk. My young friend wanted to be a comfort to me, and his chocolate milk was what he had to send. I will always be grateful for the love shown to me, my family, and for my parents.

February 26 Text to Jane: We've been putting the funeral stuff together one piece at a time in manageable chunks. I'm dreading tonight seeing it all together.

JANE: I'm sure it will be beautiful. A true testament to their love and commitment to faith and family.

ME: I hope so.

JANE: Have a little confidence in yourself. I do.

ME: Thank you but right now I don't think your confidence is warranted. (It was difficult for me to imagine that I was doing anything right.)

JANE: Well if nothing else Wayne was involved so I'm sure it is fine.

ME: He has been amazing. You have too. I'm just having a moment. Sorry.

JANE: You are entitled. No need for apology.

On Thursday night, I learned that Dara's picture had not been included in the news tribute to Mom and Pop. I had not noticed the omission when the piece aired. I had emailed a photo of Dara with Pop, one of Mom with Layton, and one with Wayne, Mom, Pop and me to the television station. The only photo they cut was the one of Dara with Pop. She was heartbroken. Friday morning, before the service, I talked with Dara. I explained that I had included her picture with Grampa. The video was more about Grammie than Grampa. The editors had what they thought was an extra photo and didn't use it. I reminded her how important she was to her Grammie and Grampa and how much they had loved her. It must have been terrible to think she had been deliberately excluded from a tribute to her Grammie and Grampa. I would never inflict that kind of hurt on someone I despise, yet I managed to do it accidently to my sweet girl. I am so sorry.

As the visitation closed and it was down to Wayne and Mary, the kids, me, and the funeral director's family, Dara and Layton came into the chapel. They said, "There's a lady out in the hall. She has been watching you all evening. She's the one who brought your Sonic drink." Jane had not only showed up but stayed through the entire night, watching, prepared to step in if I needed anything. I never had a friend like that before. A pastor friend had driven six hours across Kansas to be at both the visitation and funeral. I was completely overwhelmed by the love shown in so many ways by so many people.

February 24, JANE: Is Wayne driving you on Friday?

ME: No. I'm driving me on Friday. I could throw away a couple of Sonic sacks out of the car and invite you to ride with me.

JANE: Or you could let me drive you and I'll throw away the boys' empty pizza boxes.

ME: Unfortunately, I get better placement in the funeral procession.

JANE: A bit morbid, but good point.

Jane left her car at Plum Creek and rode with me. With all that was so far beyond my control, I needed literally to be in the driver's seat. I could not ask for or allow anyone to help me. Even then I was trying to be… I don't know, strong, brave, independent? **I simply could not allow myself to appear weak or to be weak. I was afraid of what might happen if I ever allowed myself to crumble. I have been my own worst enemy through all of this.** Jane never allowed me out of her sight all day. She sat beside me during the funeral and rode with me. As I write, I realize how self-absorbed I was. I was not taking anybody's needs but the kids and my own into consideration. Apparently, it seemed to others that I was caring for everyone else. I was trying but failing.

During the funeral, the video montage I had submitted was replayed on a loop as it had been during the visitation. The Reverend Dr. Dennis Ackerman introduced himself as having been Mom's District Superintendent. "For those who don't know," Dennis said, "I was technically Beth's boss, as if that ever really mattered." At that precise moment, a photo of Mom and Pop, where Mom hid her face behind her hand, flashed across the screen. It was as if she was answering Dennis, "I cannot believe you just said that!" I choked back a laugh.

Dennis was so focused on his notes that he did not see that picture flash by. When I told him about it, he laughed. He said that he had never been able to get the last word with Mom! He had thought surely that day he would get it, but no! She still had the last word!

It was a terribly cold day. Layton sat beside me at the cemetery, shivering, partly from cold and partly because neither of us could get warm. I wrapped my arm and jacket around him. He cuddled into my side. I was not sure whether I would ever be warm again.

The people of the Plum Creek Church served a phenomenal meal. I was so wrapped up in myself and in caring for Dara and Layton that I still don't know whether the Plum Creek people came out and ate with us. I hope they did. I am told that they did, but I have no memory. I was pretty much unaware of anybody but the kids. They were my focus and my lifeline.

When we got to the church, I saw that people were already coming out of the kitchen. They were ready to serve lunch and needed someone to give the blessing. Dennis had not yet arrived. I was the only preacher in the room, and people were starting to look toward me. I turned to Wayne in a panic. "They want me to do the prayer, and I…just… can't." He assured me that someone else would surely handle it. Just then, Dennis walked in, saw that everything was ready, and called the group to prayer. I am deeply grateful that Dennis made it back in time to offer the blessing.

After lunch, my cousin came by the table where I was sitting with Dara and Layton. Uncle George had heard that I was going to sell the farm where my parents and I had lived together for seventeen years. She didn't want me to be hasty in making this decision. I never said anything about selling the farm. I never even considered it. It is part of Mom and Pop's legacy to Dara and Layton. People will make assumptions like that about what you are thinking, feeling, and planning. I am grateful Robyn chose to ask me rather than keep the rumor alive.

Plum Creek loaded us up with more than a week's worth of food. I brought mine home and put it away before going back to handle the flowers. There were so many. We sent some to local nursing homes and some to the senior citizens center. We held back a plant for each family at Plum Creek who would like to have one. The people of the Plum Creek church were so important to my parents that Wayne and I wanted to honor that love. We brought home the rest of the flowers and plants.

I know people have been worried about me being home alone. They seem not to understand that I really am an introvert. I function well in large groups. When I need to look out for me, I do it alone. I need to find secluded space and time to recover. The visitation was tough. More than 400 people came. They had no idea how draining that much contact is for me. I don't mean to complain. I appreciate that so many came to show their love. It is just that their presence, the sheer numbers of them, took a toll on me.

Friday evening after the funeral, Jane texted to check in: Hey.

ME: Hi. I cannot tell you how much you have carried me this week. "Thank you" is a totally inadequate phrase, but it is all I have. Got home at about 5:00. Watching an intellectually stimulating "The Simpsons" marathon.

JANE: It's what family does. Sounds totally fascinating.

ME: About my speed right now as I look through the cards that came in today's mail. I'm feeling honored and blessed by the outpouring of love last night and today.

JANE: Your family has touched many lives.

ME: Still this response has been overwhelming. When both of the preachers at the service and the funeral director wipe away tears, my parents had a powerful witness and impact.

JANE: Absolutely. You and Wayne aren't half bad either.

ME: Thanks. It feels strange to say, but today was a good day. My parents would have been pleased.

JANE: It's not strange. I think they would have been amazed at how many lives they touched. I wonder if your mom might have enjoyed a little making Dennis stutter.

ME: Not a little! It would be a point of pride.

JANE: I'm sure.

ME: Mom would be surprised by all the people who turned out with expressions of love. She sometimes doubted she had made any difference at all. I trust she knows better now.

"It will get worse." I resented it when my friend, Dorothy, said that on the morning after the accident. She was right. It does get worse. In the immediate aftermath, there is so much busyness and business to be attended to that you don't have time to let the loss take hold of you. At the same time, your mind seems to take a holiday. It shuts down to protect you from acknowledging something which is too painful to handle. Friends and family gather around immediately. After weeks, sometimes months, friends have done their consolation work and moved on with their lives. Eventually the business of the funeral and the estate is finished. The mental fog begins to clear, and it is time to sit and realize what and who you have lost. With no one around, or only a faithful few, it gets worse. Only after this time of worse and much worse, is it possible for life to get better.

I am a reader. I have read everything I could find on grief. I searched for a timeline or mile-markers, some way to know when this overwhelmingly painful period would end. I have found no such timeline, no mile markers. There is no map. I have done extensive online searches on grief, grief recovery, how introverts handle grief, etc. You may come to call me "Google Girl." You will find many references to the Elizabeth Kubler-Ross five stages of grief in your own reading. Take them for what they are worth to you. There were no answers there for me. Some speak of the stages of grief, as though you can check them off, "denial… accomplished," "anger… done," etc. Others call grief a circle where there is both forward motion and backward. My own image is that of a yo-yo. I quickly plummeted to depths of sorrow, hurt, and fear. It took much longer to climb back up the string. Then came another plunge, sometimes as far down as the first time, sometimes not. Climb back up, but not necessarily all the way. Down and up, down and up, always seeking that equilibrium point where it would all stop and life would become normal again. I have yet to find that point.

A friend offered to make remembrance pillows for Dara and Layton if I would bring her some of Mom and Pop's t-shirts. Knowing little about making pillows, I had no idea how much material she would need. I took Lindsey two shirts each from Mom and Pop. She made three pillows and four teddy bears. I gave two of the pillows to Layton and Dara, and a teddy bear each to Wayne, Dara, and Layton. I kept a bear for myself and named her "P.A.M." P.A.M. is an acronym for "Pop and Mom." I usually call her "Pammie." The third pillow went to Uncle George on the first anniversary of the accident. I have spent a lot of time cuddling P.A.M. She still rides in the car with me.

I once believed that at one year the deep grief would end. Surely, I could not hurt like this for more than a year. **On February 22, 2016, I heard Dorothy's words again. "It will get worse."** I had spent over a month feeling better. I had gotten caught up in the office. I was enjoying time with my friends and family again and going to family events. It even felt good again to be in the pulpit. I thought the worst of the fog was in the rearview mirror. I was so wrong! On the anniversary of my parents' deaths, it seemed as though every inch of progress

I had made was gone. **I was back in the depths of the fog.** The weight of that fog was as crushing as in the first days after the accident, maybe even a little worse. That may sound silly until you are in the middle of your own fog. Grief fog has real weight, and you will come to understand just how heavy it is. The good news is that the renewed fog did not last nearly as long this time. **I know that days of overwhelming grief will come again. I also know that they will pass. And they will come again. And they will pass.**

That One Friend

You need to find that one friend with whom you can be completely honest. I have felt such guilt and doubt, but the preacher in me simply could not show it. Jane knows my whole story. She has been with me every step. She even offered to come and make faces at me when I appeared on TV. She would have accepted nothing less than total access. **If you have someone who loves you enough to let you speak of your loss as often as you need to, you are most blessed.** If you do not have such a person in your life, find her (but not Jane, she's mine!!)!

On May 4th, I attended a workshop which our church requires of all pastors. The topic was ethics and boundaries. Leaders explained how the pastor should not rely on the congregation to care for her. It felt as though they believed everything I had done with the two churches over the preceding three months was absolutely wrong. "If you must be a weepy mess," they said, "do it somewhere else." "Do not let your congregation care for you or expect them to do so. It is your job to care for them and not the other way around." This troubled me. I texted Jane.

ME: I have put way too much on you the last couple of months. I am sorry for that but also grateful that you let me. Thank you.

JANE: That is what family does. We support each other.

ME: I have been counting on you though more than is fair to you. I did not mean to do that.

JANE: I did not see it that way. You are too hard on yourself. I was honored you allowed me to be there.

ME: Please let me know if I ever cross the line with you or if you see it happening at the church. I am busily second guessing every decision I make right now.

JANE: It is a natural state to be in. You keep holding yourself to such a high standard that you have to just rush through the grieving stages. Just let it come as it comes. And if you do cross the line, I'll let you know.

ME: Thank you. It is just hard to be sure of anything right now. Be my brain for a while until mine comes back online.

JANE: That may not be such a huge improvement. You might want to reconsider.

ME: See, you are already covering for me!

The 2015 Great Plains Annual Conference was conducted in Wichita, about 180 miles away. The accident was within fifteen miles of my house, but I have to make short commutes every day. I think I transferred my fear of being in the car to long trips. I could not go to Wichita without leaving some information for Wayne…just in case. I checked in with Jane.

ME: I need to ask a favor I hope not to need.

JANE: Okay. Shoot.

ME: I am not planning, desiring or expecting to collide with a roadside barrier along I-35 this week. You just never know. If I am not here on Saturday evening to tear it up, would you tell Wayne I have left him a note? It has pay on death instructions for my financial stuff, the lawyer to contact to wrap up my practice, and some other instructions. I plan to tear this note up on Saturday with no one else ever knowing it existed. I just can't leave for Wichita without knowing I have things covered.

JANE: It is a bit morbid but given recent history completely understandable. Yes. I will handle it.

ME: I know. Sally Sunshine will return to regular programming tomorrow. Thanks Sis.

As my parents' fiftieth wedding anniversary approached, I got stuck. I could not get motivated. It was difficult to write sermons and nearly impossible to do any work for my clients. I had many responsibilities but no capacity, a fact I hoped I was hiding well. I wasn't.

ME: I'm stuck today. I have my to-do list, but I am not working on it.

JANE: You can work on my to-do list.

ME: Thanks! I need to work on mine, I'm just...not.

JANE: What does your list look like?

ME: Two items each day for a week and a half. I thought making manageable chunks might help. I want to be current by the end of June. I am learning that I have to move slowly sometimes. But I have to keep moving.

JANE: The turtle and the hare both make it to the finish line. Stop playing "Trivia Crack" and get to work.

ME: Nag, nag, nag. Such a big sister!

JANE: That's my job.

ME: Yay you! Project 1 done.

JANE: Great. Now don't stop. Just roll into the next thing and you'll be so high on yourself you'll roll into tomorrow's list too.

ME: Hee hee hee. You are on a roll today! And I am on page three of my five page answer. You...you're good you.

JANE: Well let's look at this shall we. I am over here sweating in the hot sun. Nearly fell off the ladder but that is another story. Back to you. So I'm sweating blah blah and YOU. You're chilling in an air conditioned office playing "Trivia Crack." What part of this equation looks equitable????? Hmmmmmmmmm???

ME: I'll have you know that I have not played "Trivia Crack" in over 15 minutes… oh withdrawal. Second, don't text and climb. I've warned you about breaking you. I won't stand for it. Third, I like chocolate ice cream. How's that?

JANE: Ummm. I'll have **you** know I nearly fell for no reason. Just standing there. No text. Just oooppps! You started out pretty okay but fell in a rabbit hole at the end. Too bad. You were so close.

ME: I was trying to distract you from your equity claim. How did I do with that?

JANE: Epic fail.

ME: Project 2 done! Client coming at 2:00 to pick up. May make enchiladas for supper to celebrate. And if I'm gonna fail, at least it was epic!

JANE: True. So what task on tomorrow's list are you gonna do until your client comes at 2:00?

ME: You do wonders for my self- esteem. "Lame at new levels." "Epic fails." How did I ever get along before we met? You broke up my pity party about an hour ago.

Periodically, I have had complete shutdown moments where I dreaded even leaving the house. Most of these fell on or near the twenty-second of the month, the "monthiversary" of the accident. In September, I had made plans with Jane and her family. At the last minute, I backed out.

ME: I am sorry to have bailed out on our plans. This has been a shutdown weekend. I am looking forward to a time when I can accept your invitation. Thanks for the invite and the patience!

JANE: No problem. Some days are better than others. This too shall pass. Allow yourself to cry when you need to. Be a hermit when you need to. Be angry and scream when you need to. There's no script. No map. Each person's journey is uniquely their own. Be kind to yourself.

ME: I do not know what I ever did to deserve you, but I would be happy to do it again! Thanks!

JANE: The feeling is mutual dear. I am blessed to have you in my family.

Christmas came about ten months after the accident. I expected myself to participate in all of the needful Christmas rituals at full strength. I kept pushing for the return of some sense of normalcy that never came. Two days before Christmas, during a really tough Advent season, I checked in with Jane.

ME: Good morning! If you have a few minutes, I'd like to ask you a question.

JANE: What's up?

ME: Do you think I am placing unreasonable expectations on myself?

JANE: You want the long answer or the short answer?

ME: Yes!

JANE: Short answer is yes. Long answer is yes. You only allow yourself little pockets of time to grieve. To heal. To be angry. To let your emotions out of the box. You keep the lid on so tight. It is almost like you make yourself schedule an appointment to have emotions. You would never treat another human, even a human you don't like, the way you treat yourself.

ME: I honestly don't see any other way to do this.

JANE: It is hard. I just know you are trying to organize and schedule your grief. To plan it. This says to me you are trying to control it. It is not something that can be controlled. It has to happen as it comes.

ME: I feel so out of control. My response to this horror is all I can control.

JANE: Do you feel like your approach is working? I'm guessing no since you asked.

ME: I just don't see an alternative. I can't just curl up in a ball and hide.

JANE: Why not? Maybe not a week but you don't have any commitments until tomorrow. And after Friday you have over a week before you have to go back to work. Even then you are the boss.

ME: A boss who is at least two months behind.

JANE: Would not being behind at work help you feel that you have time to let go?

ME: No. That is just an excuse, added pressure. Really, I am just afraid that if I let myself fall apart, the pieces will never come back together.

JANE: They won't come back together the same way. And that is not a bad thing. Right now, you are broken. When the pieces come back together it will be a new you. One without gaping holes. It will be like your own resurrection.

ME: I know. I understand. I just can't make myself believe it.

JANE: This is where faith and trust become difficult. You must have faith that whatever God allows you to endure will bring you through the other side healed. I love you.

ME: You must to put up with this basket case twin of yours! I love you too!

JANE: Trust me, I have seen basket case. I've worked with basket case, and you are not close!

ME: If you had seen the display of the past couple of hours, you might rethink that assessment!

JANE: Or I might applaud. See you just never know!

ME: You win! I surrender…just this once. Don't get used to it!

Jane has allowed me to be whatever I have needed to be, do whatever I have needed to do, and say whatever I have needed to say without judgment. I only wish that everyone going through the fog of grief had such a friend. And that she has unlimited text is a bonus!

Help!

Please do not be afraid to acknowledge that you need professional help as you grieve your loss; a pastor, counselor, or therapist. There may be things you do not feel free to tell your family or your friends, things you fear might cause them pain, but things that you need to say. It took me a long time to be able to make an appointment with a grief therapist. I thought it showed that I was weak. I thought it would disappoint my mom to see that I am not strong enough to handle my grief on my own. I was wrong. I finally realized that without help, I would never be able fully to live again. In July, I checked in with Jane.

ME: I'm going to go through Pop's desk. Baby steps but a first step.

JANE: How is it going? I can come help this week.

ME: I just copied the computer files to a flash drive. I thought if I started with the financial, less personal stuff I could claim making a start. So, I've made a start. Today I will have made a four foot by three foot start. In four months, I have made a twelve foot start. Yay me. Wayne will come down when I need reinforcements. Right now I am trying to stand on my own two feet.

JANE: Okay. Don't be too much of a stud. I'm here if you need me.

ME: I know you are. Thank you. If the financial files are this rough, I don't know when I'll ever get to the personal. Based on the size of the house and my rate of progress, I should be done in about 55 years.

JANE: That works. Gives you something to do when you retire. Don't want you being bored.

ME: My hands started to shake when I found Pop had stashed a copy of my college graduation photo where he could always find it.

JANE: You were close. You do know that won't be the only surprise you find.

ME: Depending on how "strong" I am, I may go download Mom's computer to a flash drive. Then all of the household, church and preaching records will be on my computer.

JANE: Can you handle all that in one sitting?

ME: I'll know in a couple of hours. Sometimes stubbornness is helpful.

JANE: It is.

ME: Maybe today is the day.

JANE: Guess you are going to find out.

ME: I need to start making "our house" my house.

JANE: Yes you do. Otherwise you will always have a cloud hanging over it.

ME: Do you know anything about Juanita Bartel, a therapist in Olathe? I'm thinking about seeing somebody and found her info online.

JANE: I know a couple of people but none in Olathe.

ME: I don't even know if the question is appropriate yet. Think I'll try some dolphin therapy in Galveston next week and see how it goes.

JANE: If you have thought about it, it is probably appropriate. But dolphin therapy is good too.

Five months ago today, we buried Mom and Pop. Today I began grief therapy. I never thought I would be in therapy. I have too many questions and things to work through to put on Wayne or Jane. So, I looked up a therapist online, Juanita Bartel, a Christian grief counselor. We connected right away. I asked her for a timeline of normal grieving though such a thing is impossible to predict. She said that generally months four through ten after a loss are the period of most profound grieving. Five months is right on track to seek help. She told me that normal grieving lasts from eighteen to sixty months. The first year is typically experienced as numbness. In the second year, grief really hits. True. In the third year, real healing begins. Those are round numbers and estimates, but they tell me that I am not abnormal. I desperately needed that. She closed our first session saying, "Be gentle with yourself." If I am completely honest, I have to admit that I have no idea what that means. I certainly do not know how to do it. I have tried to push my way back to normal. I have such a sense of responsibility... so many things that I must do. Be gentle with yourself. Friends have been telling me not to be so hard on myself, not to hold myself to such a high standard, and to allow myself some time to fall apart. **Be gentle with yourself.** Right! How?

ME: Good morning. What do you think the churches will think of my seeing a grief therapist? Won't change my decision. I'm just trying to foresee issues.

JANE: Why does anyone need to know? You do have a right to some privacy. I know you are kind of an open book but you can keep some stuff for yourself.

ME: If you don't think that is something at least the Pastor Parish Relations Committee needs to know, I'm okay with that. Just initially felt like I was hiding something significant.

JANE: Why is it important for them to know?

ME: I don't know. Just a feeling. That is my place for accountability to the churches. I may be way overthinking this. I tend to do that.

JANE: You have been very honest and accountable every step of the way. Therapy involves your innermost emotions. The raw ones that are sometimes scary. They belong to you and nobody else. It is like remodeling a house. It doesn't look great at the start. During the process sometimes it looks better and sometimes worse but the end result is great. If someone were to examine each step or only see certain phases it might look like it's getting worse rather than better. Sometimes you have to break it down to rebuild it on a more solid foundation.

ME: That does not sound like much fun.

JANE: It is not easy. But the end result is worth it.

ME: I'm counting on it.

I need help. I need someone to talk to who has to listen, someone who won't be upset by the memories my stories evoke. I have put too much on Jane over the last several months. She has been so supportive, but I can't keep dumping my emotional stuff on her. It is not fair. And she is a member of the Pastor Parish Relations Committee (PPRC). I have just forced her to compartmentalize what she knows from our friendship from things she is obligated to share with the PPRC. I have made a royal mess of things.

Session two with Juanita. We went deep fast. Juanita did a genogram. We just went back to Grandmother and Grandad and Grampa and Grandma. She said we have a lot of grief work to do. Someday I will be ready to re-invest in life, but I am nowhere close. I said, "Okay." She sensed hesitation because she said, "What does that mean?" I told her about my two month renewal leave, that by September, at least publicly, I have to be okay. **She said I cannot allow anyone to put time limits**

on my grief. Grief is experienced in proportion to the love of the one lost. She said she was sure I could put the grief on a shelf while preaching, or I could allow this to become my ministry. I am frightened that I will not be able to come back the way I need to, the way I am expected to, more correctly- the way I expect myself to.

Nearly a year after the accident, I finally had the courage to tell my churches that I was still struggling, and that I had chosen to seek professional help. The sermon was titled, "Good news." It is based on Luke 4:18-21 (NIV). *Jesus chooses this passage from Isaiah as his text as he prepares to drop a bombshell. "The Spirit of the Lord is on me, because he has anointed me to preach good news to the poor. He has sent me to proclaim freedom for the prisoners and recovery of sight for the blind, to release the oppressed, to proclaim the year of the Lord's favor. (Luke 4:18-19 NIV)" I can imagine this dramatic pause as Jesus very deliberately rolls up the scroll, hands it back to the attendant, and sits down... Everyone waits... eager to hear what Jesus will do with this passage. And he does not disappoint. "Today, this scripture is fulfilled in your hearing. (Luke 4:21 NIV)"*

We can be imprisoned by certain personal circumstances that never place us in an actual cage but which nonetheless take away our freedom. Every day, people are imprisoned by depression, by addiction, and by other illness. These things make people prisoners in their own minds, and bodies, and beds. Jesus came to offer freedom to these prisoners. I am a little bit nervous to tell you this next part. I have been seeing a grief therapist since the end of July. We are working on "complicated grief," the complication being a double loss in a sudden accident and no ability to see the bodies for that final time. The reason I bring this to you is that so many people, and I used to include myself in this number, believe that a Christian can never be so hurt or broken that they need to seek professional help. That simply is not true. Scripture says we do not grieve as those who have no hope (1 Thessalonians 4:13

NIV), but it does not say we do not grieve. Sometimes, we need help to experience and express that grief. Jesus says, in this passage, that he comes to proclaim freedom to the prisoners. Those imprisoned by grief, by mental illness, by depression. Those imprisoned by physical issues. Sometimes, he simply speaks peace to the broken heart. Sometimes he sends healers into our lives. Sometimes he leads us to seek out those healers. But, make no mistake Jesus comes to proclaim freedom for the prisoner, whatever our prison might be. I am grateful that he led me to a Christian therapist with whom I can share those things I simply can't unload on you or on Wayne. Those things that I need to say but have no sanctioned place to say them. Jesus brought me the freedom of this caring Christian woman.

Jesus came to release the oppressed. And to proclaim the year of the Lord's favor. It seems silly to mention it now, but my family New Year's tradition was to stay up fairly late. Sometimes we would make it to mid-night. Other times, when we were ready to call it a night before mid-night, we would simply watch the festivities in another time zone and go to bed. At about 11:30 on December 31st of 2015, I realized that I had to stay up into the New Year. I felt compelled to see the end of 2015 and let it know that it had not won. Silly, right? It seemed so to me even as I was driven to see the old year out! And I claim the year of the Lord's favor. Even in the loss of 2015, and it was extraordinary, I was so blessed. I found the deep love of friends both here and across the country and on Facebook. I have felt the support of countless prayers. People I counted as kindly associates proved to be friends. Friends proved to be family. God has deepened my faith. I am incredibly glad to see the end of 2015, but I still proclaim it as a year of the Lord's favor, and I can do it with a straight face.

I do not know what I would have done if I had not sought out Juanita Bartel. As a lay pastor, I really have no pastor to whom I can turn. Wayne was suffering the same loss. I did not feel that it was right for me to add to his pain the concern that

I was not making it. I felt this incredible sense of responsibility to my churches to be strong enough to allow them time to grieve. Juanita has become my lifeline, my sounding board, and my friend.

As one who struggled with the idea that seeking professional help showed weakness, let me reassure you. It is better to recognize your need for help than to struggle needlessly. There is someone who can help. Please seek out that help if you need it. **You do not need to be ashamed.**

The Timeline

The First and Second Months

I was back in the pulpit before I was able to return to my law office. At the March 3rd clergy meeting, we heard from a speaker on disaster response. He kept saying that the survivors of a tragedy would have to get used to a new normal. At least, that is what I heard. Finally, I could not take any more. I left the room, went into a nearby classroom, and sobbed. I have no idea how long I was gone. When I had regained my composure, I saw that he was still speaking. I texted Jane.

ME: The clergy meeting is on disaster response. I bailed out after the third repeat of "they'll have to get used to a new normal."

JANE: Well that sounds super fun. So what disaster are you supposed to be prepared for?

ME: Anything from a house fire to a tornado that wipes out half a town. Could involve just one family or hundreds.

JANE: How exactly does one prepare for that?

ME: He just kept saying help is gonna leave. The locals will have to stay and learn to live in a new normal.

JANE: What is that supposed to mean?

ME: I don't know. I bailed after "new normal." I am well aware I am moving into a new normal. I just did not feel the need to be on display to the entire district as I did so.

JANE: I'm not sure how you practice for tragedy. So were you feeling the message was specifically for you?

ME: I knew it was not targeted, but knowing and feeling don't have to match.

JANE: I hear ya. People mean well but you still can't help feeling that you are being stared at.

ME: Wayne said I got the good seat Friday (at the funeral). He felt very much on display, while I was hidden in the curtain.

JANE: Agreed. People ask if you are doing okay. And they really want you to say yes. Because they don't know what to do if you say no.

ME: Couple that with the fact that I am not a public emoter (probably coined a new word) and eventually there will be a private but major meltdown. I'm sorry. TMI.

JANE: I think it is a new word. It will happen. Tears are a release. You've had to hold it together and tend to matters at hand. We're sisters. TMI does not exist.

ME: Okay.

JANE: Please don't shut me out. I want to be here because I love you.

ME: I'm not. How do I explain to you how I'm feeling, when I can't define it myself? It has just been a really rough day.

JANE: You don't have to explain anything. I can only imagine. You are human. Just because you are a preacher doesn't mean you can't allow yourself to be angry or sad. Scream. Throw stuff. Cry. You don't have to be strong. You've done enough.

ME: I feel proud to be their daughter, guilty that they were on the way home from meeting me when it happened, and terrified of an unknown future. Thank you for giving me permission to lose it. I was withholding it from myself. No sarcasm there. Sincere thanks.

JANE: Sometimes the things we givers say to others, we don't say to ourselves.

ME: I do know that I am not alone.

JANE: Helpers think they have to be strong all the time. The moment we allow ourselves to be weak is the moment someone will need us. That's the fear. But we always forget the flight attendant rule. Put on your own oxygen mask first so you can help the rest of the passengers. Of course you are not alone. If you fall off the planet for too long I will stalk you. And I'll bring Dorothy with me.

There was so much that had to be tended to in the first month after the accident. There was the funeral and dealing with the insurance company. I was not only back in the pulpit but also leading Plum Creek through the season of Lent toward Easter. It is all a blur. People were so generous with me, realizing that I was doing the best I could. I seem to have been the only one who found fault with my performance.

As a preacher going through the season of Lent with two congregations, I was able to keep busy the first seven weeks after the accident. I just kept moving. I have heard that a moving target is harder to hit, and I was trying to avoid getting hit again.

April 4 JANE: Are you sleeping?

ME: Nope. What's up?

JANE: No. Are you getting sleep?

ME: Sometimes. Not much this week.

JANE: Should I sing you a lullaby?

ME: Think I just need to get through tomorrow. Did I miss something in the service last night? Act tired?

JANE: You didn't miss anything. Just wondered if you were sleeping. Why will tomorrow make such a difference?

ME: I needed to take the churches through Lent, for Mom and me both. Tomorrow (Easter) I'll have made that. It is a milestone.

JANE: Got it.

ME: I'm thinking about taking a couple of Sundays off in April. Bring in a speaker not related to either church. Give me a break. Give Plum Creek a chance to consider whether they really need and want me or need someone else.

JANE: You think they just said they want you but really don't? Or is it too hard to stand in that pulpit?

ME: Neither, but they are still trying to come to terms with not Beth. Someone else in the pulpit might make it easier for them to heal. They see me, they see Mom. I need to give them time and a little space to decide what is best for them. I was readily available. I don't think they ever even considered another possibility.

JANE: Good point. They didn't get a chance to heal.

ME: I am just making stuff up as I go along. I do not know the right answer for them or for me. You asked an innocent question, "Are you sleeping?" And you get all this by way of reply. That'll learn ya. You will love this. The renter for the farm wants to plant corn this spring. That is right, the queen of the corny joke is about to become a corn farmer.

JANE: You are not supposed to know. It is a process. I think your idea is solid. And FYI I ask because I want to know. And your jokes are not getting any better.

ME: Maybe with a new crop?!

JANE: Umm… no.

Two of the songs I used for the Easter services were songs we had used at the funeral. David Phelps' "End of the Beginning" and "Victory in Jesus." I made it okay at Princeton but about lost it at Plum Creek. I had Easter lunch with Wayne his extended family. I left early. I came home and crashed on the couch. The next morning, Jane texted.

JANE: Good morning sunshine. What is on the agenda today?

ME: I intend to make and consume a pitcher of iced tea, because I think it is important to set goals. Otherwise anything I accomplish today will be purely accidental.

JANE: Way to keep it attainable.

ME: In my defense, it is a big pitcher! Plum Creek refuses even to consider someone else. They say that conversation takes place if and only if I tell them no.

JANE: Just don't let them guilt you into taking the two point charge if you don't feel you are able. And don't do it out of a sense of obligation to your mom. It has got to be what you want or it won't work.

ME: Right as usual. I do want to do it. I think it could be good for all of us. It will take some time to be sure, but I am hopeful.

JANE: Well duh. Of course I'm right. My natural genius should have given that away. But I did go to school for this kind of thing.

ME: So, you are ganging up on me with the natural brilliance and training. I cry unfair!

JANE: Again. Duh. I thought you were a faster learner than this.

ME: Not on the Monday after Easter. Remember my lofty goal for the day? Now who is not paying attention?

JANE: Oh I heard you. I just felt you set the bar too low and I am trying to help you challenge yourself.

ME: Good luck with that. Today a full pitcher of tea is the sum total of my ambition. Better luck tomorrow.

JANE: Then I live to fight another day.

ME: I give up. I'll add one. My renter just showed up. I'm going to watch him make circles in the front yard with a disk and maybe even a planter. Better? Dive into your list. Have a good day. I am fine. Really. Talk later.

JANE: Okay. Have a peaceful time gazing... Mom is at Fontana post office today if you are bored.

ME: I appreciate it. Just enjoying some down time. I really need to hit it hard in the office this week. Tomorrow.

JANE: Yes. Procrastinators unite tomorrow. I am a member of that club.

ME: Usually that would be true. Last week I did a Bible study and five worship services. I am just tired. I'll renew my dedication to the procrastinators club in the morning.

April 13 ME: Bad day. When I picked up Pop's death certificate, it read cause of death "thermal injuries" and "smoke inhalation." We were praying that they had not burned to death, but he did. (From what I have been told by people who were at the scene, neither of them was conscious when the fire started. There was smoke in Pop's lungs. It was devastating to learn that he was still alive.)

JANE: Man. I was afraid of that. It seemed odd to me that his certificate was taking longer than your mom's. I am really sorry. Can I do anything?

ME: Not really. Thanks. I think I just found the trigger for the meltdown I have been expecting.

JANE: It was bound to come dear. Now is as good a time as any. Let me know if I can do anything.

ME: I will. Probably check in with you tomorrow.

An April 29 email: I appreciate your sharing your heart. My tendency is to bottle up emotions. I don't do loss well, and this is the biggest I could ever imagine. I'm trying to figure out how to write and then give a Mother's Day lesson using the phrase "Mom was," rather than "Mom is..." I knew that phrase would enter my lexicon someday but not today. Mom was always the one who helped me sort through the difficult things, and now her death and Pop's is the hard thing I have to sort through. I find myself questioning and second guessing every decision I make.

And you are right about the question, how can the world keep spinning when mine is off its axis? I know how to smile at the proper time and laugh when someone tells a joke, but it is meaningless. I know the right answer when someone asks, "How are you?" It is not a true answer, but it is the "right" one. During the United Methodist Women's District meeting, the district officers presented me with a memorial gift, a very pretty plant and rustic planter. As I carried it to the car, several women commented that I had really hit the jackpot with my plant. My first response, which I managed to stifle, was "If you could erase February 22nd from the 2015 calendar, so that my parents were still alive, you could have this stinking plant!" My verbalized response was, "It is very nice, isn't it?" I think people don't always hear what they say.

The Fourth and Fifth Months

I thought I was more ready for the Memorial Service at Annual Conference than I actually was. **There are so many firsts, and this is the first Annual Conference Mom and I haven't attended together.** The visiting Bishop, it seemed to me, used the question "Is God with us or not" as the springboard to a political statement. He barely mentioned the dead in the Memorial Service, but he certainly had a political agenda. I was angry. I talked with friends about it, but they had not heard the sermon in the same way. Maybe it was just me.

Sitting in the hall during a break, a friend came over to offer his condolences. I was still reeling from the fact that Pop's death certificate showed he was alive when the car caught fire. I told my friend about the death certificate. His son was on the scene, and he had said that there was no way my parents burned alive. They were dead long before the fire started regardless of what the coroner might say. The news was oddly comforting.

June 18 Facebook: I am having a weepy mess sort of a day. It has been almost four months since the accident, and I am emotionally paralyzed. I have a ton of work to do for the office and for the churches, and I cannot make myself care. This is not progress! Shouldn't I at least be able to function by now?

ME: Hey, I'm having a weepy mess kind of day. Make plans then back out. I'm sorry.

JANE: Wanna talk?

ME: Just missing them both more than I can handle at the moment. This too shall pass, right? Right?! That was one of my often ill-fated attempts at humor.

JANE: Yes. It shall pass. Not as soon as you like I'm sure, but it will pass. And ill-fated is kind of an understatement!

ME: I think it is a combination of Father's Day this week and their 50ᵗʰ next week.

JANE: That would do it for sure. It's a lot to happen in a short time frame.

ME: Less than four months since the accident: Wayne's birthday, Mary's, ours, Mom and Pop's birthdays, Mother's Day, Father's Day and their anniversary. I am about done "celebrating." I don't know yet just what, but I'm going to do something special on their anniversary.

JANE: That is a lot of celebrating. The special thing sounds like a great way to honor their life together.

June 19 JANE: How you feeling today?

ME: About the same. I'm somebody who plans. And I do not know what is next. So, I can't plan for it.

JANE: This will be a new journey for you. A lesson maybe. How to live without certainty. Without a plan. It may bring you closer to God. To have to fully trust Him and His plan because you don't have your own plan. Maybe???

ME: Wow! It is going to be a tough lesson for someone who keeps a master checklist of my checklists. But I think you are absolutely right.

JANE: Yea. I kinda surprised myself on that one. Every once in a while I have a really good brain moment.

ME: It is not so rare as you make it out to be. I know people keep saying this is all normal, but I keep worrying that it is not.

My mind is the one part of me I could always count on. And it has hit the showers. I fear that it won't come back.

JANE: Your mind has not changed. It is the same. Your spirit has been damaged. Not broken but damaged. Bruised. Fractured. Bruises heal. Fractures heal but it does require time. If you do not allow a broken or fractured bone to properly heal it will always cause some level of pain or discomfort. If it heals you can look back upon the break, the thing that caused the fracture but it will not consume you. It becomes another part of who you are.

ME: Thank you for the analogy. It helps. I just get scared sometimes.

JANE: I know. We all get scared and for much less than you have endured.

June 20 JANE: How's it going?

ME: Over the past four months, the feelings of being overwhelmed have come and gone. I have been immobilized for three straight days now. Maybe this is progress. I don't know.

JANE: Anytime you get up and move, it is progress.

ME: Thanks. I think you are right.

JANE: Duh. I know I'm right. I don't say stuff just to hear myself talk.

ME: Okay. I'm going to say something you have been longing to hear…you win.

JANE: Booooh yah. That's right!!!!!!!

June 21 JANE: How's it going?

ME: Okay. I figured out how to celebrate Mom and Pop's anniversary. I am asking people to post special memories on Facebook. I think everyone who participates will enjoy reading the stories. Also, I am bringing donuts to both churches Sunday.

JANE: That sounds like a great idea.

On June 21st, I requested that Facebook friends share memories of my parents in honor of their fiftieth wedding anniversary. It is important to share memories as often as you can and as often as you need to. In doing what seems necessary to you, you may also be helping someone else.

June 30 JANE: Good morning.

ME: Hi Sis. You know, I always called my mom on the way home. I didn't call the afternoon of the accident. I think I had decided to surprise them by getting home early. I just realized that the time I would have called was almost exactly the time of the accident. I think God waved me off calling. I would have always believed it was the distraction of my call that caused the accident. God spared me that. He is good. I guess that answers the how ya doing today question. I think last interactions are left to the interpretation of the survivor. If there is a way to find our behavior blameworthy, we tend to take it. I know I had the phone in my hand and for some reason did not make the call. I did call about an hour later, about an hour before the deputies arrived. No answer, so I assumed they had stopped at Wayne's leaving the phone in the car.

July 5. I am not going to preach for the next two months. After church, I went to the Sirloin Stockade for lunch. I had not been there since the accident. The table where we sat that day was open when I walked in, highlighting my sense of emptiness. That table was the last place I saw them. I started to type "saw them alive," but that is the last time I saw them, period. The greeter met me at the cash register with a hug. She had seen the accident report on the news. She told me how sorry she was, and that Mom and Pop were nice people. We had met at that Sirloin Stockade every other week after church for more than five years, so my parents were well-known and well-loved there.

I decided to follow Mom and Pop's route home. It took me twenty five minutes to get to the crash site. They crashed at about 2:35, so they left the restaurant at about 2:00. They spent a few minutes at the church on the way. I had left at 1:45, so even if I had stayed to figure out what to have for supper, it probably would not have made any difference. They would still have had time to get to the crash site by 2:30. **I need to know more about their last moments. I just don't know if I can deal with what I will learn.**

July 12. ME: Hey, I have got some large memory gaps from February. I'm trying to fill some of them in. I know this is a dumb thing to fixate on, but did we visit on the way out to the cemetery and back or listen to the radio?

JANE: We talked. I don't even remember the radio being on.

ME: Thanks. I spent a good portion of the day on automatic. I think those are things I need to be able to remember. So the book will be complete of course.

JANE: No kidding. You may not remember everything, but it is normal for people to block out chunks of time.

ME: Thank you. I think with me part of the desire to know is vanity. Did I acquit myself well when I needed to? I want to remember the reasons people kept saying I was strong. Because strength was not a factor. I simply did what was necessary. Not really strength but survival. Questions about that week have been bothering me, but I just now have the nerve to seek the answers.

JANE: People think you were strong because you did not cry in public and you kept a sense of humor. And because of the enormity of losing both parents at once.

ME: You mean I got credit for my lame sense of humor? Well I guess there had to be once.

JANE: That was probably your only time. People look at a traumatic situation and say to themselves, man I could never do that. So when you did it you looked like Wonder Woman. People were in awe you weren't curled up in the fetal position in a corner.

ME: Fetal position was not an option. I'm not that limber! But really, even now I cannot imagine doing anything differently. Nobody saw how you were carrying me. Nobody saw you watch over me at the visitation. I think I am remembering the stuff that matters after all. Some of the details can remain just details. Thank you!!

On July 22nd, I looked at my sermon from February 22nd, the last sermon of mine that Mom and Pop ever heard. If I had known they would be dead six hours later, would I have said something else? Or did I need to have this particular message of hope to find just five months after I lost them? The sermon is based on Genesis 6:1-22, 1 Peter 3:18-22 and Mark 1:9-13, all taken from the NIV.

Good morning! Today is the first Sunday in the season of Lent. Our first step in preparing for the celebration of Easter is to remind ourselves to trust in the Lord. We also remind ourselves this morning of the signs of God's covenants, the rainbow and the cross.

The sin of the world had grown so vile, so widespread, and so overwhelming that God could no longer tolerate its presence in His world (Genesis 6:1-22 NIV). Does that description make you wonder whether I am talking about Noah's day or ours? I happen to be talking about the Genesis account, but the description sounds pretty familiar, doesn't it? There was only one man who continued to follow God. God allowed Noah to save a remnant of God's creation by building an ark and taking selected ones aboard. We know about Noah and the flood. Every land animal that was not on the ark died. I say it that way, because a flood doesn't necessarily kill off all the fish but is pretty hard on air breathers!

Eventually, the waters subsided, and it was safe to venture out of the ark. When Noah and his family left the ark, they immediately made a sacrifice, a burnt offering to thank God for His protection during the Flood. God was pleased by the offering. It showed that Noah was still God's man. God told Noah that He would never again destroy the world in a Flood. God placed a rainbow in the sky, so that God and man would always be able to remember God's covenant. Today, we can still look to the rainbow and know that we are under the protection of that covenant. He didn't say anything about snow and ice, but no destruction of the world by Flood!

The Scriptures talk about a second covenant, one where all who are accepted into it and who accept it, receive salvation and eternal life. Peter writes, "For Christ died for sins once for all, the righteous for the unrighteous, to bring you to God." You are saved by "the resurrection of Jesus Christ, who has gone into heaven and is at God's right hand- with angels, authorities and powers in submission to him. (1 Peter 3:18-22 NIV)"

The sin of the world in Noah's day was merely a reflection and an extension of the first sin in the Garden of Eden. There instead of listening to God and honoring His one prohibition, Eve listened to the serpent and ate of the forbidden fruit. She compounded that sin by convincing Adam to try some too. From that moment on, the perfect creation of God was stained with sin. And not even the washing away of humanity in the Great Flood of Noah's time could make the perfect creation clean and perfect again. No, from the time of humanity's fall in the Garden, an ultimate solution was required. And God alone could make the sacrifice necessary to make it work.

We don't know how long Eve debated with the serpent, but I doubt that it took him forty days to convince her to try a bite of the already enticing fruit. The tempter did his work well, and eventually Eve broke God's law. She then shared her sin with Adam, convincing him to try some too. This is humanity's first sin. This is the reason an ultimate solution was required. This is why we have the passage we read this morning in the first chapter of Mark.

In Mark 1:9-13 (NIV), things were about as good as they could possibly be for Jesus. He had honored His Father's law by being baptized in the Jordan River. As he came up out of the river, Jesus heard the voice of God say, "You are my Son, whom I love; with you I am well pleased." This must be as close to Eden as a human being had been since Adam and Eve were evicted from the Garden.

So, to answer for Eve's temptation, Jesus was sent into the desert for forty days of testing and temptation. Jesus' faith and his commitment to honor His Father never wavered during that forty days. Jesus answered every temptation. Once Jesus had answered for our temptations, angels came and cared for him. Jesus had answered for temptation, but that was not the ultimate answer, not the complete solution. More would be required to erase the stain of sin.

The second covenant, the ultimate solution, the key to eternal salvation is symbolized in the cross of Jesus. The cross is the sign of the second covenant as surely as the rainbow marks the first. When we see the cross, we are reminded that the price of sin has been paid for all who are willing to accept it. And in the cross, God remembers His ultimate solution to the problem of sin. We trust in the Lord to keep the promise of salvation.

The Psalmist says, "To you, O Lord, I lift up my soul; in you I trust, O my God. Do not let me be put to shame, nor let my enemies triumph over me. No one whose hope is in you will ever be put to shame, but they will be put to shame who are treacherous without cause. Show me your ways, O Lord, teach me your paths; guide me in your truth and teach me, for you are God my Savior, and my hope is in you all day long. (Psalm 25:1-3 NIV)" We know the signs of God's great covenants, and now the Psalmist calls us to trust them. The Psalmist says, I offer my life to you, O Lord. I trust you completely, so lead me wherever I should go. Teach me whatever I should know.

In our recent Bible study, we have been reminded that it is easy to trust in the existence and goodness of God when everything is going right, and we are feeling well. When things fall apart, and life begins to hurt, that trust is harder to come by. When we have all that we need, it is harder to tempt us to sin. When we are in need, the greatest temptation is a low risk sin that would satisfy that need.

Yet, when things get bad and we know that we are not strong enough to make it through on our own, we begin again to trust. We remember, "No one whose hope is in you will ever be put to shame. (Psalm 25 NIV)" When we need God the most, we revive our trust, which in turns strengthens our hope.

I invite you to keep the cross of Jesus constantly before you as we go through this season of preparation. Let that image remind you to give up your doubt that God loves you beyond all measure and beyond all reason. Give up your fear that somehow God might fail to honor His promise of salvation. Give up your fear of sharing the gospel of Jesus Christ with a friend.

Four years ago, on Good Friday, as I left the church after an Easter Egg Hunt and worship service, I turned on the car radio. The first song on the radio as I left the Good Friday service was "How deep is your love?" It is an old love song by the Bee Gees. I immediately asked myself the question, how deep is Jesus' love? It is as deep as a nail driven into a tree, as deep as a scourge across the back, as deep as a spear thrust into the side, as deep as a cold, cold tomb. How deep is His love? As deep as the eternity his children will spend with him. When even the radio conspires with God to remind us of His love, maybe, just maybe we ought to pay attention. The nails, the scourge, the spear all remind us of the cross of Christ. And in an undeniable way, that cross reminds us of the depths of God's love for us.

Having seen God's love manifested in so many ways, and being reminded even by old love songs on the radio, how can we not trust in the Lord? We know His love for us is amazing. And the gospel lesson *we read this morning tells us that after the period of temptation, Jesus went out into Galilee. This was his message and should be ours, "'The time has come,' he said. 'The kingdom of God has come near. Repent and believe the good news! (Mark 1:15 NIV)'"*

Trust in God. Sounds so simple, but there is so much power in the phrase. Trust in God with all that you have and all that you are. Trust and then step out in faith. Amen.

I looked back at that February 22nd sermon again on April 1, 2016. The message brought tears to my eyes, reminding me of my dear parents and my loving Father. **I still trust Him.**

The Sixth and Seventh Months

Juanita said that months four through ten were generally the period of most profound grieving. The sixth and seventh months after the accident proved her right, at least for me. **The six month anniversary of the accident tore me up again.**

August 22. Facebook post. The accident was six months ago today. I'm sitting in the living room, the walls stripped of the art work we put up when we moved to the farm. Tomorrow, Wayne is going to help me put up new pictures. I have new furniture coming. To all outward appearances, I'm moving on, doing okay. And when I come back to the churches in September from a much needed renewal leave, I will be publicly okay. I'm not. Nothing seems right. I miss Mom and Pop terribly. I hope and believe that they are at peace, but I admit to being selfish enough to want them back.

August 23. Facebook post. Thank you for all of the supportive comments on my post yesterday. The six month anniversary hit hard. I had hoped that yesterday's meltdown would be more in the nature of Applebee's "Triple Chocolate" than boo hoo waaah waaah. But, being the classic "overachiever," I ended up doing both! Well, you know me...

On September 9th I went to Wichita for a meeting of the South Central Jurisdiction Mission Council, an agency within the church. I packed up early so that I could leave as soon as we were done. I could not find my room key. Since I rarely sleep in a motel bed, I always put the keycard, with my wallet and keys, on the bed. I found my wallet and keys with no problem. I could not find the room key. I started to panic after I had searched my bag and suitcase twice each. I stripped the bed and looked under everything on the floor. I could not find the key. I even checked in the bathroom a time or two. Finally, in a panic, I looked under the breakfast menu that I suddenly remembered had been left on the bed prior to my arrival. There was the key. I sat on the edge of the bed rocking back and forth crying uncontrollably for about fifteen minutes in both relief and terror. I have always been able to rely on my mind, but it is not functioning. I have never been so frightened.

September 28. My therapy session this afternoon was quite helpful. Last week, Juanita loaned me Henri Nouwen's book, *The Wounded Healer.* I came across the following passage, "(*Wounded Healer.* Pp.72-73.) After so much stress on the necessity of a leader to prevent his own personal feelings and attitudes from interfering in a helping relationship, it seems necessary to re-establish the basic principle that no one can help anyone without becoming involved, without entering with his whole person into the painful situation, without taking the risk of becoming hurt, wounded or even destroyed in the process. The beginning and end of all Christian leadership is to give your life for others. Thinking about martyrdom can be an escape unless we realize that real martyrdom means a witness that starts with the willingness to cry with those who cry, laugh with those who laugh, and to make one's own painful and joyful experiences available as sources of clarification and understanding." And, "Who can listen to a story of loneliness and despair without taking the risk of experiencing similar pains in his own heart and even losing his precious peace of mind?" I told Juanita that I had found these passages and kept coming back to them. She asked why. I said that I kept thinking of her in this passage. How did the passage make me feel? Concerned. That seemed to surprise her. Why would I be concerned for her by these passages? From what she has told me of her own story, I know that some of our conversations have been difficult for her, hitting a bit too close to home. I do not ever want my own healing to come at the expense of her pain. I am a protector, and I would rather not get help for myself than to allow someone I care about to be hurt. Whether Juanita likes it or not, she is on that people I care about list. She does not want me to worry about her but about seeking healing for myself. I have felt that I was dumping my emotional baggage on her and on Jane to their detriment. I have felt guilty about it. I frequently worry that I am hurting people in seeking my own healing. Juanita and I talked through the fact that she was willing to take that risk. She said that when our conversations get too close, her immediate prayer is "Lord, don't let my stuff impede Jada's healing." I laughed. I have offered the same prayer for her. She said I need someone that I can talk to who will listen and understand. She is willing to walk with me on this path, and you can't do that without risk. Then she asked how long I had been worried about this. I answered, "Longer than I have had the book, but these passages crystallized the idea for me." I am glad she loaned me the book. I had been preparing to withdraw from therapy so that my stuff would not hurt her. I am grateful that we had this frank and honest talk. When we parted, Juanita made me agree to continue to work with her and not be afraid for her wellbeing. It is a promise I could not honestly make. I will continue to see her, but I will also continue to worry.

The Eighth and Ninth Months

In September and October, I was able to begin to sort out some things and make some decisions. I also began working through some of the experiences I had had since the accident, mining them for meaning. I was beginning a new way of life whether I wanted to or not.

On October 16, I met Dorothy for the United Methodist Women Annual meeting. We skipped dinner to talk about Mom and Pop and how much I still miss them. She too was grateful the other night when Jerry offered a tribute to Pop at church conference. When I heard the praise music coming from the sanctuary, I felt better. I carry my tension in my shoulders and often carry my shoulders high enough it seems I could rest my ears on them. As praise music flowed over us, I noticed that for the first time in weeks I did not have to force my shoulders down. I completely relaxed and welcomed the worship experience. The women's chorus was wonderful, worshipful, and healing. The keynote speaker was introduced. Her text was from the Book of Esther (4:12-14 NIV) "for such a time as this." I believe God was speaking through the music and the message. Mom had frequently quoted "for such a time as this" when there was some new challenge in the church that she or I or we had risen to meet. I was deeply comforted by the worship service tonight.

I worry. My prayers, fervent though they may be, seem to be getting answered no. I prayed for a successful surgery for a friend. She had complications. I prayed for her sister. Tonight, the sister suffers from complications. I worry that God has chosen for me a season of no. I do not understand why. Since I am just beginning to pray in the way that I believe God wants His children to pray, constantly and in His will, I do not understand why the answer is no.

October 30. On Monday, I bought a car. As I was pushing buttons, I discovered a sunroof. I was excited thinking, "Mom is going to love this!" Then it hit me, Mom is never going to see it. I miss them both so much. Sometimes, I think I am going to lose my mind. I sit and brood. I don't cry much. This pain in my heart constantly reminds me that I will not see them again in this life.

November 5. I found my Carmen CD containing the song "Heart of a Champion." I realized that it has been a long time since I have had the heart of a champion. I have been frightened and weak, but not a champion. I have felt like quitting. I have felt deep sorrow. I have felt tremendous guilt. I have not felt like a champion. **As I listened to that track, I realized that it is time for me to reclaim my champion's heart.** God has made me to succeed for Him, to find joy in Him, and to be at peace with Him and His plan. And I am more often able to laugh freely, to enjoy little things, to be productive in the office. **I am just coming to understand the level of faith necessary to find the good in tragedy. I saw it clearly enough early on to point it out to others but not to see it for myself.** Even writing that does not make sense, but then, not much has made sense in the past few months.

I posted in November that I would be teaching a weekend lay servant seminar; my first solo teaching since the accident. I admitted nervousness, because my mind is still not very clear. Well-meaning people started writing about how smart and capable I am and how well I will do. I appreciate their desire to build me up. I do. People don't realize how, with every accolade, I feel more pressure to succeed.

I remembered comments from friends in the church as I was preparing for the Bar Exam. One said that he was not one bit worried. Of course he wasn't losing any sleep. It was not his future on the line! The second, one with a well-earned reputation for always saying the wrong thing said, "I know you are worried about this test. I will be praying for you." I made a beeline to Mom's office and said, "Our friend just spoke to me about the Bar Exam." Mom said, "Oh honey. I am sure she did not mean it!" Grinning, I said, "I hope she did. She said she would be praying for me." Sometimes, I need someone to tell me that it is okay to be afraid. It is okay to acknowledge that I might fail miserably. Sometimes, I need to hear that it is okay to not be okay. And nobody seemed to get that then or now. I know that I am not the only one feeling like this. I am not the only one who has ever suffered such an incredible loss. I know this, but I feel alone. I feel as if no one understands or could understand what I am going through.

Then on Monday afternoons Juanita shares her woundedness with me. It is the greatest gift she could give. If your therapist has the strength to share their own wounds to help you heal, you have been given a great gift. When I hear Juanita's story of loss, I know that I am not alone. It helps to see how she is living with her grief. She is an amazing person with a strong faith. She serves others and encourages us. Juanita gives me hope. She reminds me that God is still God, that God is in charge, and that God is working in my life. No one else knows how to tell me these things in such a way that it truly connects. I thank

God for directing my Google search to her. I thank God that she agreed to see me.

November 13. At 11:00 this morning, I finished writing the class I am presenting tonight. When I got to my class, it was clear that God had heard my prayers. The class consists of a group of friends and students from around the Conference. Most are taking the class for the simple reason that I am the teacher. They love me and want me to do well. I am grateful. This evening's sessions were going to be the most difficult, and they turned out to be fun.

The Tenth and Eleventh Months

Ten months after the accident, I was finally ready to ask some of the questions that had been plaguing me. I did not have the nerve to do it sooner. I simply was not ready. Now, I needed answers.

December 2. I may have made a terrible mistake, but I need to know. I called the Sheriff's Office this morning to request a copy of the accident report. I will pick it up in an hour and a half. I don't have any idea what I may find in the report. I don't know whether I will be able to handle it. I know that I feel driven to see that report. There are so many unanswered and maybe unanswerable questions.

December 3. I did not go to bed last night until after 11:00. I feared that I would dream about the accident, but I did not. I tried to have one of my pseudo sessions with Juanita, the kind where we have a deep conversation, but she is not even present. I found that I could not even talk to her. Mom and Pop were so badly burned that it was impossible at first to make gender identification much less to identify the crash victims. So many friends prayed for me yesterday for the strength to find answers from that report. And I did learn some things. I am grateful.

On December 4, Jane texted that her mom was coming to the soup supper with her. Sue wanted to see me, to see how I am doing. I had supper with Jane, Sue, Dave and Kaden, and a friend from church. They let me tell stories about my parents. They let me say the things I needed to say. They let me share, because they love me. I am so blessed to have such women in my life. And Dave and Kaden gave us time to talk.

December 5.

JANE: You have your mother's gift of gab. I felt as if I closed my eyes I was listening to her tell stories. I know she is proud of you, because I am.

ME: Thank you. Thanks so much.

JANE: Absolutely. I only speak the truth. I love you Sis.

ME: Love you too.

This afternoon, there was a holiday service of remembrance at Eddy-Birchard Funeral Home. Every family they had served in 2015 was invited. They reminded us that our grief is our own. We should not allow it to be manipulated or timed by others. They gave each family a Christmas tree angel with their loved one's name and life dates on it. As each name was called, one member of the family was to stand and receive the angel. Wayne had me stand up for Mom. Layton came with his dad, and he looked up at me as I stood for Mom. When I sat down, I asked, "Would you like to stand up for Grampa?" His eyes lit up, "Yeah, I really would." "Do it." Layton received Pop's angel. I am proud of both kids. They each knew what they needed to do with regard to the service. Layton needed to come. Dara needed not to come. They were both right.

I knew that this weekend was going to be difficult. I got Juanita to see me twice this week. She encouraged me. We talked about what I so feared about the Christmas store. I acknowledged that I was afraid I would fail. I thought that I needed to be strong enough to allow others room to grieve. I was afraid that I would be overwhelmed by the emotions surrounding the ministry event my parents loved so much. I was afraid that I would cry and spoil a joyous day for others.

January 1, 2016. I did it. I survived the year Mom and Pop died. I would not necessarily have made that bet, but I did it. Now to learn how to live again. I went to the cemetery yesterday before going out for a New Year's Eve supper. I started with Pop. I told him how much I love him. I want him to be alive and with me. My heart literally hurts for him. I love my daddy and I want him back.

It took a lot longer talking to Mom. I have learned a lot of things in the last year. I have always lived with the dread of disappointing Mom. I know she had to set high expectations of herself in order to survive polio. She always said that she could kick herself in the side and do whatever needed to be done. Anyone who did less was a disappointment. I apologized for disappointing her. I wish she could put her arms around me one more time.

At the restaurant, I was seated one table from the spot where I took the Mom hiding her eyes picture two years ago. I had three pictures of that New Year's Eve supper on my phone and looked at them often throughout supper. I had a book of daily devotional readings for healing after loss. I read several and ordered a steak. I took a selfie with P.A.M. and posted it to my Facebook page. I did everything I could to imagine having Mom and Pop there celebrating the New Year with me. Every time I looked at the pictures, I smiled. I left a $20 tip on a $30 steak. It felt good to be generous like Mom and Pop were.

Leaving the steakhouse, I went over to Starbucks for a Chai. I covered my ticket and the guy behind me. There was $2 left over for the barista for a tip. It felt good to be generous. On the way home, sipping that wonderfully hot Chai, I thought about Juanita and her idea of ice cream grace. She says that life is like a full meal. There is so much going on. Grace, like ice cream, runs down over all and fills in the gaps. I think I like the analogy of Chai better. Not only does it pour over everything, like ice cream, but it warms you as it goes. My heart has felt so cold since the funeral. I like "Chai grace."

At eleven months, I was rapidly approaching my self-imposed deadline for recovery from my grief. Yes, I know now how ridiculous that sounds. I believed I would have used up everyone's grace for me by then.

January 4, 2016. I asked Juanita to help me explore the emotional side of grief. I have been trying to think my way through grief rather than to feel it. I am frightened by what I might learn about myself. I know I need to do this in order to heal. I think Juanita understands me even better than I do. I believe that she will help me to feel my feelings and not be so afraid of them. I am frightened by a lack of control. I am frightened by a world in which my foundation has been shaken. I am frightened now that Mom and Pop, who were always there for me, can no longer back me up. I am working without a safety net for the first time. I cannot allow this to make me timid. I have to keep going. Juanita asked whether I thought I had realistic expectations of my ministry. I think I am doing better. Yes, I imploded on Christmas Eve, but I did ask someone to preach for me on the anniversary of the accident. Juanita was proud of me. She knows that it is hard for me to ask for help.

January 18, 2016. Kathy called this morning to see if they could come by and pick up Pop's truck. I asked her to call Wayne. I could not be there when Pop's truck was taken away. I couldn't drive the truck. I had no real attachment to the truck. But... it was Pop's truck. That mattered more than I had ever dreamed possible. I held Pammie and cried for half an hour. I left the title, death certificates and a truck key, garage door unlocked, and the air compressor outside, and I ran away. I have let Wayne handle a lot of things this last year that were simply too hard for me.

One Year

Despite all that I had read, I still believed that one year was some sort of game changing milestone. I will never forget my parents. I will always love them. After a year, though, I expected that I would be able to charge into my new normal and fully live again.

I expected that the actual day of the anniversary would be difficult for me. I had no idea how to prepare. **We know how to prepare for birthdays and anniversary celebrations, but the anniversary of a devastating loss? How does one prepare for that?**

On Monday morning, the anniversary of the accident, I was crying while looking at Facebook when Jane texted me. Very simple. Just, "Thinking about you today, Sis." That really started the tears. I was so off balance all day. I took Uncle George his Mom and Pop pillow. He sat and hugged it the whole time I was there. I am glad that I brought him the pillow.

I spent most of Tuesday sitting quietly. At about 4:30 I went up to the cemetery. I had told Mom and Pop I would come back. I do not believe they hear me, but still I had made a commitment. I did not want to lie.

I am still trying to figure out this be gentle with yourself stuff. I am learning not to push myself so hard when I need to just sit and remember. I did not go to the office the week of the anniversary. The week off, I thought, could do me some good. I hoped that I could come out of the fog enough to spend a day writing. **I don't know.** That seems to have become my slogan over the last year, "**I... don't... know.**" I hate that, because my identity has always been wrapped up in being the person who knows stuff. I am so tired all of the time. After a week off, my head did clear some. The fog lifted, because I took the time to allow myself room to grieve.

There is still a lot for me to learn. There are still a lot of tears to be shed. There are some wonderful stories yet to be told and laughter to be shared. **One year after your loss is not a grief ending date. The anniversary will have an impact.** I do not know how, or in what way, but I am certain that it will. The next day, you will wake up. The sun will rise. You will go on, because that is what life is. Getting up and going on.

Learnings

Don't try to Rush back and Don't Push yourself too hard

I thought I would be able to go back to my office right away. For many, bereavement leave is only three or four days. I took the week off after the accident, but I had planned to be back the next week. I badly overestimated my resilience. The visitation was on Thursday night and the funeral on Friday. The following Tuesday I knew that I was not yet ready to go back to the office. I had no capacity to go back to a law practice where I create estate plans so soon after losing my parents. It was three weeks before I could go back to the office. It took nearly a year to get back on track if even now I am back on track.

This advice comes from the do as I say not as I did files. I believed that I needed to be back in charge of myself and fulfilling my responsibilities immediately. The accident took place on the first Sunday of Lent. I felt responsible for both Princeton and Plum Creek. I could not let the churches go through the season without a pastor or with substitutes. Weather forced the cancellation of services at both churches the week after the accident. The following week I was back in the pulpit at Princeton. The week after that I began preaching at Plum Creek as well. As I write this, the sheer arrogance of my belief that no one else could lead the churches through Lent is staggering. These churches are my extended family, and I needed them probably more than they needed me. I could not have been much of a preacher or a minister in those first weeks. Somehow, we staggered through together.

I would like to believe that if I was forced to make these decisions again, I would choose more wisely. I would like to think that I would not be so driven again. I would like to think that I would have done the right thing both for my churches and for myself. But, I know me. I could not have done any differently than I did. I could not leave my churches abandoned. I needed to be with them. I am grateful to my District Superintendent for seeing my need to be with both Princeton and Plum Creek. I am grateful that he permitted that combination of churches to take place.

You too will have some opportunities for self-care during this time. Take as many of them as you are able. **Know yourself well enough to know what you have to do and what you are able to do. Love yourself enough to say no when the task ahead seems to be overwhelming.** You alone know what you need. You have to be willing to accept help and even ask for what you need. There will be friends, relatives, and the Church all willing to help you. They simply do not know how or what to do.

What do you Really Believe?

I do not know how non-Christians survive such a time. Even though I could not always feel them, I know that I was constantly being lifted up by praying people. **Even when God seemed silent, I knew, in a place deeper than my intellect, that I was not alone.** Without the loving support of my church family, I do not believe I would have made it through that terrible first year. The faith we shared kept me going even when the words sounded empty. I still knew that the promises of God were true.

On March 15, 2015, three weeks after the accident, I preached for the first time in Mom's pulpit. It took two months for me to come to see Plum Creek as my own congregation. This is part of that first sermon. *I know victory might be the furthest thing from our minds. We may not be feeling victorious. We are in mourning. We are grieving. Let me assure you, as one who knows, when we look to the cross of Christ, we will find our victory, our healing. The blessing to be found in the accident is that it proved to me that I really do believe all the things about God that I have always claimed to believe. I have always claimed to believe that God so loved the world that He sent His only Begotten Son that whoever believes in him would not perish but have everlasting life (John 3:16 NIV). I have always claimed to believe that there is salvation in the Name of Jesus. I have always claimed to believe in the loving, compassionate presence of* the Holy Spirit in all circumstances, our Comforter in times of trouble. I have come to understand that you can only truly know that you believe what you believe you believe when that belief is tested. Follow that? I will always miss my parents. But I have not one shred of doubt that they are presently enjoying the fulfilled promise of salvation that we all claim to believe. Not one shred.

What do you really believe? **When there is nothing left but faith, we discover whether our faith is enough to sustain us.** This is not to ask whether God is enough, He is. This is about whether your trust in Him is deep enough for you to allow Him to carry you. There are several versions of the poem "Footprints in the sand." The most familiar shows only one set of footprints during the difficult moments of life. It was then that God carried us. Another version builds on that idea. At a certain place along the path, there is a jumble of footprints overlapping and making swooping circles. It was there that God healed us, and we danced together. Truthfully, my favorite version shows one set of footprints and two long deep furrows. It is there that God dragged us toward healing kicking and screaming. Even though I believe in God and trust in Him, I still leave a lot of heel marks!

You are so Strong!

Strength is a family trait and a personal expectation for me. I have wanted to be strong enough to protect my family and my churches. I needed to be strong enough to continue in my ministry and my law practice. Yet, every time someone mentioned how strong I was, it cut like a knife. I knew that I was not feeling strong. I was feeling terrified, alone, and desperate. I see strength as a noble characteristic, and nothing about my situation felt noble.

When the sheriff's deputies came to tell me about the accident, they asked me to sit down. They had no way of knowing how I would respond to the news they brought. I would not sit down. I could not sit down. I have thought a lot about why. I realized that, in my mind, to sit down would show weakness. That was not acceptable to me.

The night of the accident, Wayne invited me to come to town and spend the night with him and his family. I refused to leave home. I had a strong sense that if I spent that night away I might never be able to come back. That night, I stayed at home... alone. I spent part of the night on my couch, part on the sofa in the living room, and even a couple of hours in Mom's recliner. But, if this was to remain my home, I had to stay.

On Tuesday, while Wayne and I were working on the funeral arrangements, I got a call from Monica Evans, a reporter from

Kansas City Fox4 News. She wanted to interview somebody in the family about Mom and Pop, primarily Mom I soon discovered. I agreed to meet her at the Plum Creek church. While the videographer got lights and sound set up, Monica and I chatted. I told her about Mom and Pop and their deep love for the people of Plum Creek. She looked at the photo she had asked me to bring. She said that I looked a lot like Mom. Then she said, "you are being very strong." I grinned and answered, "I'm faking it."

(Mom and Pop, Wayne and Jada on Father's Day. This is the photo I showed to Monica Evans.)

Everything I read, and everything I hear says that the grieving process lasts at least a year. By the way, I REALLY hate the phrase "grieving process"!! I don't know if I can keep this up for a year. I'm going about doing my thing one moment, and then something comes up. I start to cry. I know the accident was less than five months ago, but I am nearing the end of my rope. By the time I go back to the churches in September, after a two month renewal leave, I will be expected to be okay again. I should be fine. I should be able to act like I am fine. By then, I can't let on anymore how devastated I still feel.

I drive by the cemetery every day on the way to the office. I often stop. I know Mom and Pop are not there, but where am I supposed to go? What am I supposed to do? Jane tells me that I have to get used to not knowing, to not being able to plan. I think she is right. I know I have never felt more lost and alone.

One night in July, there were severe thunderstorms all around Miami County. Wayne called, and Jane texted to be sure I was okay. I have never feared storms before, and I am not sure "fear" is the right word to describe what I felt that night. I have never feared storms, because Mom, Pop, and I were always in them together. Together we believed that we were invincible. Without them I feel pretty "vincible."

I go to meetings at the church and in the district and conference. People ask how I'm doing. I give them the correct answer, but I don't know whether the correct answer will ever be true again. I'm fine. Why wouldn't I be? I mean it is not like my entire world came apart four and a half months ago, right?! I wish people would be honest. If they don't really want to know how I am, I wish they would not ask. And if they do care, I wish they would pursue it when I give the correct answer. But, truly, few ever follow up.

Self-care was a real issue for me even before the accident. I do not see myself as important enough or worthy to be paid special attention while I am grieving. This has been an issue on which the District Committee on Ordained Ministry has challenged me time and time again over a dozen years. "Why don't you take time for self-care?" Because I do not have the time. "Aren't you worth the effort to care for yourself?" Not above the people entrusted to my care. I need to work this idea through, but for today, I am simply filled with sorrow. Sorrow that I have not been in worship in a month. Sorrow that I do not feel a loss at having missed worship. Sorrow at still feeling an overwhelming sorrow. "Why don't you take time for self-care?" I struggle even to understand the question. I do not value myself or my needs above the needs of the people who need me. I cannot justify taking time for myself to rest, to grieve. It seems self-indulgent.

I have tried to understand why people push me to take care of myself. The churches looked to me immediately for leadership and pastoral care. And everyone spoke of how strong I was in the loss of my parents. Each adds a tremendous weight and sense of responsibility. How can I break down when so many are looking to me as a pillar, a model? Publicly, I have to be okay now. I live in this tension of those who want to care for me and want me to take care of myself and my own sense of responsibility always to put the needs of others first. I only attended worship three times during my nine week renewal leave. What troubles me most in this is that I did not miss being in church. I have always been in church, but I simply did not want to go. So…I just did not go.

November 16. God is so good. On the way home from a productive therapy session, I heard a new song by Casting Crowns, "Just be held." The first stanza captured me. It spoke to my broken heart the message that I do not have to be strong all the time. The song says that when we are overwhelmed, we can let go of our own need for control and just be held by God.

A month ago, if I had heard this song, I would have thought, "but they just don't know how bad it hurts." Tonight I was ready to hear the song. I was ready to hear it because of my therapy session. I had talked about the façade of strength I have put on since the accident. Juanita asked why I felt I had to be strong. It is the model I have.

I invite you to be strong enough to allow yourself to fall apart when you need to do that. Be strong enough to ask for help when you need it. Be strong enough to cry. Be strong enough to seek ways to get your needs met. **It takes a strong person great strength to admit when we are not okay. Be that strong.**

Unexpected Outbursts

Soon after the accident, there was a meeting at the Princeton church. I was getting supper on the way when the tears hit so suddenly and so fiercely that I could not see. I sat in a local park and sobbed. The tears hit with a terrible force. Until that moment, I had thought I was handling my grief. NOPE! As pastor, I am responsible for the opening prayer at meetings. I knew I could not do it that night. I texted Jane. Would you do the opening prayer tonight for the board meeting? I'm not in very good shape right now.

JANE: Yes, I'll do it. So what's going on? I wondered if it was a bad day since I didn't hear from you…Why don't you just stay home? The world won't come to an end if you miss a meeting.

ME: On the way to the church.

JANE: Turn around and go home.

ME: Can't.

JANE: Stubborn.

ME: And your first clue?

Jane prayed the opening prayer in my place, but I <u>was</u> <u>there</u>. I was almost totally uninvolved in the meeting, but I was there. Later I texted Jane: Home. If you are up to it, I'll spill my tale of woe.

JANE: I'll be around.

ME: It hit me hard this afternoon when I realized that the last thing I said to Mom was, "I don't have time (for you)." I needed to get to Princeton for the study, but Mom wanted me to take a minute and plan supper. I said, "I'll be home as soon as I can. I just don't have time for this right now." She never said anything like that to me.

JANE: Not that you remember. Memories tend to be selective.

ME: I know, but it was her nature to make time for people, especially Wayne and me.

JANE: She probably did not think twice about it.

ME: You are right. Just seems pretty selfish for a last word.

JANE: But would it seem as selfish if it weren't the last word?

ME: Regardless of timing, it wasn't my finest moment.

JANE: I'm not disagreeing with you. But it likely wasn't your first or only not finest hour. It is the timing that makes it feel more awful than it is.

ME: Yeah. Thanks. I can't fix it. Need to quit wallowing in it.

JANE: Wallowing and processing are not the same thing.

ME: True…Thank you.

JANE: You are welcome. Just remember you have to allow yourself to grieve. Don't shut it down when it comes.

Grief will often hit with a vengeance and unexpectedly. There is no preparation possible. Just know that it is coming and will eventually pass. Hang on tight and ride it out as best you can. Remember, it… will… pass.

Three-time Orphan

On May 31, 2015, I preached on Nicodemus from John's Gospel (3:1-8). I use the New International Version as my source for sermons and study. *When we meet Nicodemus, he is a member of the Jewish ruling council. And he has questions about Jesus that only Jesus can answer. The council is aware of Jesus' teachings, and they do not like what they have heard. For a member of the Sanhedrin, the only acceptable interaction with Jesus is to try to undermine him. But, this is not Nicodemus' agenda. Something about Jesus has stirred his heart. He has real questions. Nicodemus needs to know whether Jesus really is the Messiah that the people have been awaiting for so long. Nicodemus knows that his colleagues on the Sanhedrin would never approve of such an inquiry. So, Nicodemus has snuck away in the night. He needs to meet with Jesus alone and unseen.*

There are times when our needs and our questions are so deeply personal and so personally important that we cannot ask them in the presence of others. Sometimes we need to get alone with Jesus in prayer to ask the deep questions. Are you the One? Are you even there?

I think I was standing in Nicodemus' sandals not so long ago. I posted this on my Facebook page. I wrote it before I was sure I would be able to speak it. After the accident, God felt so distant and so silent. Even in the midst of all the prayers and support, I have never felt more alone. Intellectually, I knew that God was still present, still loving me. Sometimes, the things we know in our heads do not make it all the way to knowledge of the heart. I grew up in the church. I have always been in Sunday school. I know the right words to say about my faith and when to say them. And even when I could not feel them, I still believed them... at least intellectually. I knew the correct answer to the question, "How are you doing?" The correct answer was not always the true answer, but you already know that. I was still feeling like a three-time orphan, Mom, Pop and God, all gone. My entire foundation had crumbled. And I was lost.

Looking at Nicodemus' story, I think I begin to understand him better. Nicodemus was a theologian, a Bible scholar. He knew the theology of the Messiah. He knew how the system of religion worked. Nicodemus' head held most of the answers he needed. His heart still deeply needed to know whether Jesus was the One. Was he for real? Did he have the answers Nicodemus needed? This is where I found myself on a Saturday afternoon at a restaurant in Olathe as I prayed, "Are you still there, Lord? Will you show me your presence?" On the way home, every song on the radio seemed to say, "Just ask me to prove I'm here. I will always be with you. I will never leave you." And, in that moment, I knew, I mean knew heart and head, that God was and is real, and alive, and present. That is when the flood gates opened and the tears came. I must have been quite a sight rolling down I-35 crying my eyes out. They were tears of joy, because the foundation of faith my parents had built for me had once again proved to be solid and trust worthy. I realized that it was not necessary for me always to be strong and brave. I could be the sometimes fearful, sometimes tearful, child of God wrapped up safe and secure in His arms. I knew, heart and head, the presence of God. This was the same need that Nicodemus had. He needed to know more than the theory and theology of faith. He needed to feel the presence of God.

Are you afraid that your sin is greater than God's ability to forgive? It is not. Is your faith more a matter of head knowledge and intellectual belief than heart knowledge and peace? Ask God to reveal Himself to you in the way you most need to know Him. He will answer.

Sunrise in the Storm

I usually take the scenic route to my office by way of Sonic. On this September day, the Osawatomie bypass seemed to be the storm front. I watched the most brilliant sunrise I had ever seen. God created all colors and all beauty, and that morning He was simply showing off. It was that kind of brilliant sunrise that requires the offset of a cloudy, stormy sky to be fully appreciated. I was in awe of the rich reds, pinks, golds, and oranges of the sky. I watched golden light spread across the sky until it encountered the thunderstorm. As the sun rose, the light overcame the darkness, driving it back.

As I headed north, the sky lit up with beautiful color on the passenger's side of the car. On the driver's side, dark, ominous clouds, punctuated by sharp bolts of lightning prevailed. The light began to encroach upon the darkness, driving it back. I noticed all of this, caught up by the enhanced beauty of a sunrise in a storm. I looked into the storm and saw a faint but noticeable rainbow. I got my tea and headed for the office. In the intervening time the sun had risen above the storm clouds. I noticed that there were places where the light had been that were now darkened by the storm. The sun had risen, but darkness still prevailed.

Grief is like that. We know that the sun has risen, is rising. We are stronger and more whole than we were the day before.

We again meet the storm. Emotions rage and fight against the healing that is taking place, but the light still encroaches upon the darkness. For a time, the storm overcomes the light reclaiming for itself the progress we have made. We have to face the storm in order to find the promise offered by the rainbow. Even in the face of that storm, there is hope. God is there in the heart of that storm, not allowing us to be completely overwhelmed. Eventually, the sun outshines the storm, breaking it up and driving it away. The sun ultimately prevails because the light, the Light of the World, is stronger than the darkness.

I guess it is obvious that my first impression, seven months after the accident would be grief and facing that particular storm. How even in the midst of that storm, it is possible to see light, and hope, and the sustaining presence of God. But I also realized that this sunrise in the storm could be taken a step further.

I realized that all of life's journey and struggles are like the sunrise in the storm. Whatever the storm, the sun rises. It drives away the darkness, but sometimes the darkness comes back. The darkness cannot win, but it can prevail over us for a season. Here is what John 1:1-5 says, "In the beginning the Word already existed. The Word was with God, and the Word was God. He existed in the beginning with God. God created everything through him, and nothing was created except through him. The Word gave life to everything that was created, and his life brought light to everyone. The light shines in the darkness, and the darkness can never extinguish it." I chose the New Living Translation, because the imagery is more powerful than most other translations. The light of Christ shines in the darkness, and the darkness can never <u>extinguish it</u>.

I love the song, "The Deer's cry," sung by Lisa Kelly. It is based on "The Prayer of Saint Patrick." This song reminds me of the power of the Son to overcome the darkest storm. The song begins and ends with the same phrase, "I arise today." In order to arise, we must first have been knocked down by the storms of life.

How is it that we have the power to rise up after being knocked down by the storms of life? I arise in God's strength. I arise, because God promises to protect me even in the midst of the darkest storm. The rainbow in the storm contains the promise, Jesus is with me. He stands on my right and on my left. There is no point of spiritual attack where Jesus is not there. **With God my strength and Christ my promise, I arise today. You, too, may arise.**

Fake!

In October, I started reading Zig Ziglar's *Confessions of a Grieving Christian*. I ended up throwing the book across the room in frustration. For me, his words simply do not ring true. That he has such joy and certainty even in the death of his daughter has a phony sound. This brings me to me. I feel like such a phony, fraud, and fake. The night of Mom and Pop's accident, I posted an announcement about their deaths. I used all kinds of words of faith. They are home. They are safe. Faithful disciples rewarded. I did not feel any of that. In the last few months, I have many times spoken of their faithfulness and the surety of their reward. I <u>do</u> <u>believe</u> those things. I believe that they are well and happy and in heaven. I do not experience joy in knowing this. I claim to, but really I just want them to come home, to come to the Princeton Chicken Noodle Supper tonight, to not be dead. When I say anything else, I lose my integrity. How do I ever get that back? I feel like I have been both lying and speaking truth with the same words at the same time since the accident. The churches see me as a pillar of strength and faith. I do not feel a bit of it. I do not want to be dishonest with them. I want to tell them the truth, believing it to be the truth, so that when I really do feel Faith and Hope again it will have meaning. I am such a mess!

I told Juanita that I often feel like a fraud when I go into the pulpit offering words of hope that I don't really feel. I know that Jesus is the Hope of the World, the way to salvation. It is difficult sometimes to feel that truth. I have tried so hard for so long to protect my churches from the pain I feel. Juanita challenged me. Am I trying to protect the churches from the grief they need permission to feel? What would it look like if I told the churches that I still need time to grieve? What would it look like if I admitted to feeling like a fraud? Shortly after her husband died, Juanita was on the platform for pastoral prayer. She said, "I can't do this. I do not feel the faith we all profess today. I have doubts and questions." She enabled her congregation to gather around her and grieve with her. What would happen if I did that too? What would happen if I told the congregations about my doubts, fears, and needs? Maybe at the one year anniversary of the accident? Well, the lectionary for Sunday is the raising of Lazarus (John 11:32–45). Twice, Juanita has reminded me that before raising Lazarus, Jesus wept with Mary and Martha. The time seemed right to accept her challenge. It is All Saints Day. My sermon title is "For all the saints."

I emailed the sermon to a pastor friend to see what she thought. Was it timely, self-indulgent, or what? She told me that it was courageous, powerful, and meaty. I have to serve God to the best of my ability, and that means permitting the churches to see me whole and broken at the same time. I think that means complete honesty.

This is a portion of the sermon from All Saints Day. *It is a day to remember with gratitude those saints who have gone before us, the people who have led us to faith, the ones who have inspired us on the way, each of whom now rest from their labors. Focus on Jesus, the Scripture says. The best way to do this is to look at the example set for us by those faithful disciples who have been in our lives.*

On this All Saints Day, we see the community of faith gathered around Mary and Martha at the tomb of Lazarus. Jesus joins them there. Mary and Martha have just four days before buried their beloved brother. Lazarus had been Jesus' friend. Mary and Martha were Jesus' friends. And they were grieving inconsolably. What does Jesus do at this moment? Does he waltz up to Mary and Martha and say, "Get your acts together and watch this?" or maybe "Quit your crying, things are about to get good"? No. The one Bible verse nearly every Bible School child since the writing of John's gospel has memorized comes next. "Jesus wept (John 11:35 NIV)." Jesus knew what he was there to do. Jesus knew that by the end of the day, he would be having supper with Lazarus in Lazarus' home. Mary and Martha did not know that. Their hearts were broken, and Jesus wept. Jesus wept with his friends, because that is what they needed him to do. That is what they needed him to do even before he added the miracle of resurrection. They needed their friend, their savior, to understand and to join in their sorrow. Jesus wept. Then, and only then, do we hear, "Lazarus come forth."

Over the last eight months I have wanted so badly to be strong, so that Mom and Pop would have reason to be proud. I have wanted to protect you from the full impact of my grief, and probably also to protect myself from yours.

On February 22nd, I posted on Facebook. "I know some of you have already seen this news, but for those who haven't... My world changed dramatically this afternoon. My parents were killed in an auto accident. The knock on the door that should have been my dad asking me to let him in the garage was two very kind Miami County Sheriff's deputies with news I cannot even now believe or completely comprehend. They are gone. I have already seen an incredible outpouring of love. They were everybody's spare mom and dad, and grammie and grampa. My joy is that they were dedicated disciples of Jesus. They are home now." I wrote this message of their faithfulness and their reward, not because those were my words or thoughts, but because I realized that this was the message that would be expected from me.

*I have sometimes felt like a fake since the accident. I still have days, more of them than I care to admit, when I feel like a complete fraud, standing in the pulpit with a big smile and an assurance of faith that I don't always feel. I **know** that the faith we profess is real, but sometimes the longing for even another hour with Mom and Pop keeps me from feeling it. I am the pastor. I need to stand up front with a confidence I don't always feel. This makes me feel like a fraud. Sometimes, I do not have words of hope to share, but those are the words the congregations need to hear. So, I manufacture a hope I can't muster in myself. I am hoping to be strong for you, not to burden you with the things I think I need or the doubts that sometimes come.*

Eight months after the accident I bought a Ford Escape. On the way home from Olathe, I heard a song from Mercy Me called "Beautiful." It speaks of how beautiful a child of God is in the eyes of God. That God loves His children enough to die for us. We are beautiful. And it hit me right between the eyes. I have always had this head knowledge of the love of God, but sometimes that head knowledge fails to make it all the way to my heart. With this song, God built a bridge between head and heart.

On this All Saints Day, take a moment and thank God for your personal cloud of witnesses. Remember those who shaped your faith, and who inspire your walk with Christ. As I began to work on this message, I thought about my own personal cloud of witnesses, and how that cloud grew by two in February. I remember the faith Mom and Pop shared with me. I have wonderful memories of their love for me and for each other. I know that it is okay to celebrate their lives and love and at the same time mourn our loss. In the funerals that I preach, I always say, "We can celebrate that we will be together again. And even as we celebrate their life and their love, we experience their loss. We must give ourselves permission to miss them. It is entirely possible and right that one day you will be laughing about a shared experience with them and that you will be crying at the same time. No one has the right to tell you how you feel or how you <u>should</u> feel. You will experience this loss in your own way." I have said that a dozen times in a dozen different funerals, but I never really got it until now. I have great examples of Christian witness in my parents. And the way I honor Mom and Pop's faith and their faithfulness is to be faithful myself. I need faithfully, honestly to serve God by trusting in Jesus Christ to keep his promises. On All Saints Day, we remember those who inspired our faith. We miss them, because we love them, and we honor them today. Today I give you permission to remember your saints, your own cloud of witnesses, sometimes with laughter and sometimes with tears, and sometimes with a combination of the two. And I ask you to extend me that same grace.

Why?????

If this question has not yet hit you, it will. Why? Why did they die? Why in these circumstances? Why did I survive? All these questions are normal. Even if you do not voice them, you will have these questions, and it is okay!

I know my parents lived under God's protection. He rescued them too many times to doubt that. So, why was that protection withdrawn? **Why did God allow my mom and pop to die in a fiery car accident?**

In October, trying to work through my whys, I wrote a sermon entitled, "God does not owe you any answers." *Sometimes I preach more to me than to my congregation. I know that this message will not come across, at least at first, as good news. What we learn from Job is that God does not owe you any answers. Job has suffered the loss of his children, his wealth, and his health. He has suffered the counsel of his wife and the advice of his friends. All these things Job has suffered even though he is, according to God, blameless and upright. I hear Job say, "I just wish that God would tell me why all of these terrible things have happened to me, and why they continue to happen to me. I have done nothing wrong. I have followed God, and yet I have been afflicted. If God would just speak with me, I could ask why. And because I am such a good and faithful guy, I know that God would answer me."*

I have been asking why a lot lately. It is surely no secret that Mom had a lead foot. She had a well-earned reputation for speed. Yet, she was also a careful driver, a good driver. She just arrived at her destination quicker than most people. There were numerous times in life that Mom was mysteriously delayed in her travels by just long enough for her to avoid the multiple fatality accidents in her path. God carried Mom through two difficult pregnancies. God saved Mom from Polio, Idiopathic Pulmonary Fibrosis, and breast cancer. All these things, doctors said, should have killed her, but God had other plans. Why did He not offer one more miracle on February 22nd?

Pop had a heart condition that fifteen years ago doctors told him would take his life in less than five years. He was diabetic. As a child, he was in a serious car accident that only left a scar on his chin. God protected my father and spared his life too many times to count. Why not on February 22nd?

On October 12th, there was a terrible fire in Kansas City. Two firefighters lost their lives saving the lives of others. They had each entered and safely exited hundreds of burning buildings in their decade plus long careers. God had protected them in and from the fire every single time. Why not on October 12th?

Why? Why did this have to happen? In our human wisdom, there are no answers. There are no answers to random violence, to fatal accidents, or to other tragic losses. We still ask why. We demand to know the unknowable answers.

We still ask where was God on September 11, 2001, or during the Columbine school shooting, or the Sandy Hook school shooting. Where was God when horrific things have happened? We want to know why. We demand to know why. Are you beginning to see the gut-wrenching, soul-searching depth of Job's anguish as he demands to know why God has allowed these things to happen to him? He has been faithful. God has even commended him for his faithfulness. Why then has he been singled out for such suffering?

Truthfully, the answer, at least at first, is not very satisfying. The answer is that we are not entitled to know the answer. The answer God gives Job is, "I was there all along, even from before the Creation. I did not allow you to be overcome. I was with you. You were never alone."

The answer is that God was there when Pop lived long enough to inhale smoke but Mom did not. They were never alone. God allowed them to be together for each other and together when they met Him at the gate of eternity. God was on the planes that crashed into the towers on September 11th, and in the office buildings as they collapsed. God walked into the fire house in Newtown, Connecticut with the parents who would greet their children, and God walked with the parents who would find their children's names on the other list.

No matter how horrific the situation is, God's children never face it alone. I did not say we never feel alone. Get that distinction. It is important. Sitting on the ash heap scratching his sores with a piece of broken pottery, I can assure you, Job felt alone. He could not imagine how anyone had ever suffered or could ever suffer as much as he did. He felt alone, but God was with him, watching over him, and even then protecting his life. Job was permitted to shake his fist at heaven and challenge God. That was not Job shouting challenges at God. It was the deep physical, emotional and spiritual pain he felt. God loved him and continued to be with him, even though Job did not feel it at the time.

I think we all have had our moments when things were so bad that we just needed to shake our fists at heaven and scream. Why did you do this to me?! No amount of comforting words from friends can make us feel any less alone, any less abandoned. These words are important, and they will be remembered later. In that that moment, even surrounded by love, we feel alone. Yet, in that moment, God is still with us, loving us, and protecting us, even when we do not feel it.

Sometimes we do not get answers to our heartfelt whys. Sometimes we do not get the answers we want. Sometimes we get the answers we do not want. Sometimes we simply do not understand the ways of God. Some things we will never understand. Sometimes we do not get answers to the deep whys. Through it all, and in all of our doubts, and regardless of the questions, God is with us. God loves us. We are not alone.

Do I even Want to Survive this?

If your loss is catastrophic, you will probably ask yourself this question. Only you can define what "catastrophic" means to you. The question? Do I even want to survive this?

I have had several periods where I have felt like this since the accident. I am not saying I want to die. I don't. I just want to want to live, but I don't. I just don't care. I would be ready to leave anytime. I just don't care whether I live or for how long. I doubt that I will live to be old, and that is fine. I wonder whether I will ever care about living again.

In July, I created a trust for Dara and Layton's benefit. That same afternoon I went to Kansas City to pick up new eyeglasses. I had all the trust documents in the seat beside me in the car, including the unrecorded deed that would pass the farm to the trust for the kids. As I was leaving Overland Park, I was nearly hit by a car. I was terrified. I was afraid that in dying that day, I would have failed Dara and Layton. I prayed, "Please let me live long enough to get this deed recorded. I would be happy to meet you for lunch in heaven tomorrow, but please let me record this deed!"

In November, Juanita and I reviewed my updated intake sheet. I had prepared a new one, because my understanding of therapy had changed. I did not think the goals I had originally set were well enough defined. Juanita asked about some of my answers. I had mentioned having prepared a trust for Dara and

Layton and how terrified I was of being in an accident before I got it put in place. I told her about having a list of instructions for Wayne left with Jane for winding down my practice if something happened to me. She asked me if I was suicidal. I immediately answered, no. Last night I did some online research on suicide risk. The results were unsatisfying. There is no clear, definitive answer to suicide risk. Some of the things that are called risk factors are simply good estate planning: making a will, making funeral arrangements, and making sure there are funds available to accomplish those arrangements. I have moments when I do not care whether I live very long, and I told her that. But to take my own life is not an option. I will ask what triggered the question. I need to know how great Juanita's concern is on the matter. The thought that she considers me at risk is frightening.

November 7. I jolted awake around 3:00 am. I told Juanita two weeks ago that I was undecided at first whether to buy the Ford Edge or the Escape. I realized that in June I would be leaving a long term assignment. As a joke, and just for me, I bought the Escape as the vehicle in which I would make my "escape." She asked what else will you use it to escape? This morning, I realized that she may have taken the idea of the Escape as a sign of potential suicide. I have no intention or desire to end my life. That is number 1. Number 2, I could not do that kind of harm to Wayne and the kids. Number 3, I do not believe in suicide. Number 4, I do not have time for such nonsense. I have at least one book to write. I want to publish Mom's funeral workbook. I want to go to Dara and Layton's college graduations. I have things to do. I want to go back to Galveston. I want to go to Estes Park. I want to go to a hot air balloon rally in New Mexico. I want to drive the Pacific Coast Highway.

November 9, 2015, I asked Juanita what had triggered the question last week about being suicidal. She remembered asking. Did it bother me that she had asked? Uh, yeah! When a trained clinician with a discerning spirit asks if you are suicidal, it raises questions. I listed the reasons above. Short answer, then, "No, I am not suicidal." She answered, "I don't think you are either." In situations where there is a double tragic loss and isolation, emotions can spiral quickly to the point of suicide. It was important to ask.

November 14. "Are you suicidal?" The words stung like a slap in the face. How could she ask me that? I immediately answered, "No." No! Where did that come from? I did not have the nerve to ask. I was stunned that someone would ask such a thing of me. Hadn't she heard a word I had said about being strong? I began to wonder. What had I said that prompted the question? It has been nearly two weeks since she asked. The question still rings in my head. Are you suicidal? I have searched my heart and mind to see whether there is any trace of such a threat. There is not. I do not believe in suicide as an answer to any problem. As I told Juanita, "I do not have time for such nonsense. There are too many things I still want to do." I asked about the question a week later, and we talked about it. Juanita acknowledged that she does not think I am suicidal, but, professionally, she needed to ask. I am grateful for the question. I have considered the subject with her help and in her presence. And I have answered the question. NO!

February 22, 2016, on leaving Juanita's office, I drove to the lake. Looking at the water has always been restorative for me. It was the first anniversary of the accident, and I needed all the restoration I could find! On the circle drive that afternoon, as I killed the engine, I noted how close you come to the water. I realized just how easy it would be not to turn the wheel but simply to drive out into the lake. It frightened me to think how close I was to doing just that. I promised myself not to start the engine until I was sure I would choose to complete the circle. Three weeks later I told Juanita about the incident. I think it concerned her that I had delayed telling her.

March 19, 2016. I am frightened. I have been thinking about suicide, not about doing it, but about it for some time. I had two sessions with Juanita this week. On Monday, I had planned to review the accident photos. I have seen a few of the photos of the car, crushed and burned down to the bare metal. Those were bad. The photo array also includes photos of my parents in the car, on the road, and in body bags. These are photos I have not yet seen. I last saw my parents seated together at the table at Sirloin Stockade. Then, there is this gap to a view of closed caskets. I have felt for some time that I needed to view those awful photos. Juanita and others who knew about my plan to view the photos had been praying for me all weekend. I realized that I was only viewing the photos in order to force myself to a breakdown. I thought I needed to be so devastated that I would be forced to deal with my deepest, darkest fears and pain out of the accident. God pulled me back from that choice, though I still feel compelled to view those photos...some day. I do not believe that this drive is coming from God. I told Juanita that I had decided not to view the photos. On Thursday, we talked again about the decision not to view the photos. Juanita told me that she believed viewing the photos would have done me so much psychological harm that she would have been forced to admit me to a hospital. She did not want then and does not want now to admit me, but I would have forced her hand.

If you are wrestling with thoughts of suicide, pray and seek Godly counsel. Do not be afraid to get help. Get help. Seek hope. Talk to someone you trust. Please, for a fellow traveler in the fog.

Forgiveness Tour

Maybe I should speak of unfinished business. I have been in or much too near four church fights. In two, Mom became the target. In the other two, I managed to avoid full church fights by walking away from the looming conflict and the congregation. Some of these wounds are over thirty years old and some much younger. In October, I decided I was no longer willing to carry that anger and hurt. It was time to set it down. If I was ever to heal, I had some forgiving to do.

I embarked on what I have decided to call a forgiveness tour. I started at a church I once served. The assignment there did not end well. I sat out front and prayed for the people who worship there. I prayed that I might be forgiven for any ways I had hurt them. I prayed that I would be able to forgive those who had hurt me. I have carried that hurt for too long. I have decided to set it down.

I stopped by a church I had attended as a youth and young adult. I prayed for the hurt of hearing the pastor tell me he wanted me to leave his church. I recounted the story. The pastor thought I was trying to usurp his authority. I prayed for forgiveness for any ways I had hurt the church, and that I would be able to forgive those who had hurt me. I have carried that hurt for too long. I have decided to set it down.

After lunch, I continued the tour. I discovered that it is far easier for me to forgive those who had hurt me than those who had hurt Mom. I told God about the hurt the chairman of the Pastor Parish Relations Committee had inflicted when he asked for Mom's resignation. I named the cancer that the stress of dealing with a strong antagonist had caused Mom. I prayed that I would be able to forgive them, because I knew that forgiveness for these people was beyond my ability to offer on my own. Then I named each one, "I forgive A. I forgive B. I forgive C. I forgive D. I forgive E. I forgive F." I sat for a moment breathing deeply. I was not sure I could make the last statement, and without God's peace I could not have done it. I could not even have said it let alone meant it. "I forgive the antagonist, the leader of the band." I have carried that hurt for too long. With God's help, I have set it down.

When I was finished, my car would not start. I had to call for a jump start. The starter had gone bad. It was almost funny, so I chose to laugh. I decided I would still complete the tour. Just two more stops. On the way, I stopped at the cemetery. I told Mom and Pop that I was on a forgiveness tour and that I hoped they would be proud. I told them that I loved them. I told them that I was going to complete the tour. I prayed only briefly at the last stop (motor running). I spoke about the church fight and the pain inflicted there. I thanked God for sending a beloved pastor who became a healer for my family. I thanked God for helping me to forgive at all four churches. I quietly repeated, "Thank you. Thank you. Thank you. Thank you." I had carried that hurt for such a long time. It was time to set it down. God has blessed me greatly today. He has allowed me to be healed of the anger and pain and grief caused in those churches.

I encourage you to make a forgiveness tour of your own if you have unfinished business. If you have been emotionally harmed in a church, visit the church. It can be empty at the time. Pray for the ability to forgive those who harmed you, forgiveness for any harms you may have done, and the ability to release the pain and anger. BUT, do it at the time that seems right to you. As you have no doubt read, there is no timeline. The right time for everything is whenever you are able to do it. Only one day after the tour, I was already more at peace with myself and with my history.

First Christmas

I grew up in the church. Christmas and Easter were always big family days. The first Christmas without Mom and Pop was difficult. I spent the month of December dreading the next Christmas event. There were so many!

Looking back at the Christmas calendar for the December 11th weekend, it was terrible. On Friday, I went to the Princeton United Methodist Women's Christmas luncheon. That afternoon we prepared for the Plum Creek Christmas Store. Saturday was the Christmas store. Sunday was the Princeton Christmas Program. Dara's Christmas band concert was on Monday. There were five Christmas events in four days not to mention two Advent sermons preached. I met with Juanita twice. I needed someone not related to my Christmas activities to help me gear up for that weekend. I was on such a roller coaster during the entire Christmas season. I plunged to the depths in seconds then slowly climbed back up. I plunged again. I did not know how I was going to make it through the Christmas store. All I knew was that I had to make it through the Christmas Store.

The Christmas Store is an outreach ministry of the Plum Creek United Methodist Church. More than fifteen years ago, my father and I were dreaming of new ministries one day. When Mom got home from a meeting, we accosted her with our plan. We would invite kids from the local elementary school to donate cans of food for the food pantry. This would be their admission to shop for every member of their family. Mom was initially overwhelmed by the concept and a bit hesitant to try it. We talked her into taking it to the church, and for more than fifteen years, we have served Osawatomie families. Mom "bought" kids' food with the promise of shopping in the Christmas Store. Kids buy their gifts, visit Santa, and help church members wrap the gifts. This ministry grew into a passion for my parents. The last year of his life, Pop was our Santa Claus. Seeing the joy in shoppers' faces had prepared me for Christmas for fifteen years. I would have to engage in my parents' favorite ministry while sitting in Mom's chair... missing them. I was afraid the mountain might be too high to climb, but I had to try.

I dread the Christmas Store, an event I usually love. I will be the face of the Christmas Store. I will greet every family and shopper who comes. I will be out front feeling pretty exposed. We will be short staffed this year. One family who has been a part of every Christmas Store will be out of town. Dara won't be able to serve as a shopper's helper, since she will be running the photo shop I have vacated. Everybody will be trying to be cheery when we will all be thinking, "I wish Beth and Willis, Mom and Pop, Grammie and Grampa were here."

December 13. Christmas Program Princeton. Jane and Jamie each read a story for me. David read the birth narrative from Luke Chapter 2. Dorothy led the program for me. I knew I would not be up to it.

ME: I'm home. Two deer spotted in time to avoid!

JANE: Good deal. Glad you are home Eagle Eye.

ME: Me too! Thank you for reading tonight. Thanks to Jamie for reading. She was great.

JANE: Jamie says you are welcome, but she hasn't forgotten you still owe her.

ME: What are we talking? Hot Tamales? Skittles? You know my fee scale!

JANE: Peanut M&M's.

ME: Doable. And good to know!!

JANE: You okay Sis? You kept staring off tonight.

ME: Just had a very Christmas intensive weekend. Missing Mom and Pop a whole lot. I'll be fine. Thanks.

JANE: Okay. I'm here if you want to talk.

ME: I'm just trying to do Christmas, because it is expected. I really just want the year to be over.

JANE: That's understandable.

ME: Christmas Store was yesterday. Dara and Layton ran the photo shop for me, since I had to move up front into Mom's role as greeter.

JANE: She would be proud of you for taking over her role and making sure the Christmas store happened. The way she spoke of it, it had to be one of her favorite things.

ME: I don't know if this will make any sense, but they were very present in their absence.

JANE: It does make sense. They are all around you. The church. The kids. Wayne. The house. They surround you. Their love envelopes you.

December 14. Yesterday was hard. I think I did okay at Princeton. At Plum Creek, I gave Barbara the wrong week's Advent Wreath reading. Everybody was so kind about it. They teased me a little about fast-forwarding through Advent. During the Lord's Prayer I seemed to hear Mom's voice coming from within me. I choked back tears. I had to get it together and quickly, because I had to preach in less than five minutes.

Am I ever going to get to the place where I don't get blindsided by emotions like this?

Christmas recap. Jane and others have been telling me that I expect too much of myself, and that I am not being reasonable in my expectations. On the 23rd, I asked Jane whether she really thought I was being unreasonable. She said yes. She thinks I would not even treat an enemy like I treat myself. I cannot think of any other way to experience the loss of Mom and Pop. I can't break down. There are certain things that I am responsible to do. How can I do less? Well, that turned out to be just the beginning of the story. On Christmas Eve, I sat in the basement at Princeton in the gathering darkness, trying to get my head together enough to do the service. I did not think that the people upstairs even knew I was there. A few minutes before 5:00, Wilma came down and asked if I was okay. Without meaning to, I answered completely honestly, "Not at the moment, but I will be okay. I just need a few minutes. I will be up in a bit." I did the Christmas Eve Reverse Tenebrae and headed back downstairs. The box full of candles started to go through at the bottom. I put one hand under the box to keep from losing the whole mess.

I did not know that Wilma had seen how rattled I was. My phone started to ring. Wilma was calling from the parking lot. She was worried about me. She wanted to drive me to Plum Creek or at least ride over with me. I kept telling her no. I had to do this on my own. I knew nobody but Mom would ever really understand, but I had to do it on my own. It is the only way I know. The bottom of the candle box went completely through as I got to the car. I lost a lid in the parking lot. Wilma found a candle. I promised that I would do two things. I would text when I got safely to Plum Creek, and I would have somebody else do the service.

When I got to the Plum Creek Church, nobody was there yet. I asked a friend to do the service for me using my script. I sat in Pop's pew, tears in my eyes, as Curtis did my Reverse Tenebrae for the first time at Plum Creek. I got a lot of hugs but no questions. Everybody understood why I had backed out of the service.

Earlier, when I got to Princeton, I prayed for two hours of clarity and composure. Just two lousy hours was all I needed to be able to pull off Christmas Eve services for both churches. I did not even get forty five minutes. I have spent ten months trying to do what I have believed God was calling me to do, lead the Princeton and Plum Creek Churches. Now, on the holiest night of the year, He leaves me totally incapable of fulfilling my role. Was I ever even called in the first place? **I don't know. It was a bad night**.

The first Christmas without your loved one will be tremendously difficult. It will probably be worse if Christmas was a family togetherness holiday for you. The ones who are missing will be extraordinarily present in their absence. There are ways to soften this season. Don't be afraid to say no. Be willing to go to events and leave early. Change the tradition. Even with all of these things, it will still be a difficult season. May God bless you with peace as you go through it.

More Alive

In January, Juanita said that I looked more alive than I had in the time we had been working together. What did I think was the reason? I told her about my decision to tell Mom and Pop's stories leading up to the anniversary of the accident.

Tell your stories. It does not matter whether you write Facebook posts, tell them to friends or to a journal, but tell your stories. As I came up on the one year mark of the death of my parents, I knew the day would be difficult for me. About one month out, I began to dread the day more and more. Twenty eight days before the anniversary, I had an idea. I posted a special Mom story on my Facebook page every other day. I posted Pop stories on alternating days. Sometimes Facebook friends got bonus posts, as I thought of extra memories. About two weeks before the event, I was reading my posts. I kept smiling, because not only did I remember my Mom and Pop with joy so did many of my friends. Tell your stories. If through tears, that is perfectly okay. If it is with laughter, that is okay too. Tell your stories. It is good for you, and good for those who love you and those who love your lost loved ones. Let me share with you a couple of my stories.

Breakinapage. When I was in college, my father and I were avid Baker football fans. Most of the guys on the team had classes with me and were friends of mine. Pop and I would travel to most away games and never missed home games. When there was no church calendar conflict, Mom would go with us. The best game days, though, saw Pop and me on the road by 6:00 to get to town by 11:00. We would eat in town and go to the game. We would typically win the game and come home. It was wonderful time together. These were the days when navigational devices were printed on paper and published by Rand McNally. One weekend, the playoff schedule sent us to Lindsborg, Kansas to take on the Bethany Swedes. Pop drove, leaving me to read and interpret the map. The Kansas map in a Rand McNally atlas was printed on two pages. Lindsborg was on the page opposite my hometown of Osawatomie. Since the atlas was big and cumbersome, I set the details in my mind and put the atlas in the back seat. We were to turn north after a considerable distance travelling west across the divider in the page. We had been on the road for quite a while when Pop said, "Where do we turn north?" Some of the town names in that area were unfamiliar to me, and I could not remember the name of the town where we were to turn. I knew that it was just past the break in the page of the atlas. So "Breakinapage" stuck in my head. I said, "At Breakinapage." Pop did not know any better, so we began to watch for Breakinapage. To my knowledge there is no such place as Breakinapage, Kansas. We kept driving further west searching for Breakinapage. Finally, at a major intersection, there was a sign, "North...Lindsborg." I said, "Let's try that." Pop agreed. We made it to the game on time, but Pop never allowed me to forget the turn at Breakinapage. In fact even after I bought my Garmin, he would still ask, "Do I need to watch for Breakinapage?"

Fifth Chapter Wedding. Mom was Chaplain of Clinton Lake Ministries near Lawrence, Kansas for several summers.

One evening, the park ranger stopped by our camper to talk. There was a motorcycle group, called the "Fifth Chapter," whose leader wanted to get married. None of the churches in Lawrence were willing to have "that sort of people" in their churches. They had been denied multiple times. Would Mom be willing to do the ceremony? When Mom went to meet the couple, armed guards met her at the car. They warned Pop not to get out of the car and escorted Mom to their campsite. The groom was picking a pair of handcuffs off the best man as Mom approached. Mom would later say she had chosen to believe it was a magic trick gone terribly wrong! Yes, she knew better. The wedding site was primitive, meaning that there were a couple of picnic tables and several inches of fallen leaves. During the ceremony, the best man dropped the ring into those leaves! Everyone searched for the ring while Mom learned a bunch of new words, none of which she could use in Sunday School! In the ceremony the couple is to repeat words of invocation after the pastor. Mom began, "In the Name of the Father..." The groom looked at her, refusing. Again, "In the Name of the Father..." This time the groom crossed his arms and shook his head. Third time, "In the Name of the Father, look buddy we are going to stand here until you repeat after me. In the Name of the Father..." He glared at Mom for a moment, but he muttered, "In the Name of the Father." "And of the Son..." "And of the Son." "And of the Holy Spirit..." "And of the Holy Spirit." My mom was fearless, and she had so many stories to tell. There was rarely a dull moment.

Complicated Grief

There is a clinical definition for Complicated Grief. Some diagnose it as a mental illness called "Persistent Complex Bereavement Disorder." It boils down to a loss which is catastrophic to you. There is a lot of pain and emotional baggage to work through, and it will take a long time to recover any sense of normalcy. If you ask your doctor, that is probably not the definition he or she will give, but it works for me.

I have felt that my mind had "gone on vacation." Juanita helped me reconsider the idea. She suggested "hibernation." Hibernation is finding a safe place to rest while the winter storms rage by outside. It is a survival mechanism for the animal who hibernates. I realize that for me the better word than "hibernate" is "cocoon." The same bear emerges from the cave that went into it for the winter. The caterpillar dies in the cocoon and emerges as a whole new creation. "Hibernate" is to find a safe place and eventually emerge. "Cocoon" is about death and transformation and rebirth. I am not the same bear that entered the cave. I just hope I don't turn out to be a moth!

October 24. Earlier this week, I believed my mind was beginning to clear. I thought I was making progress out of the fog. This afternoon, (Friday) the funeral director called. It was the third time he had told me about my burial policy being ready. I had completely spaced it off. My mind is no clearer than it was. I have no memory, no attention span, and no ability to focus. I am frightened though I laugh it off. I grin and tell the churches I have the attention span of a gnat. I know that I am not losing my mind, and I know that this fog is part of grief. I need to be able to be clear and smart and strong again. **I need to be able to be me. I am not me, and right now, I am not even sure who me is, or was, or will be. I HATE THIS FEELING!**

December 7. My mind and spirit have been in such turmoil this week that I do not know what to write. Do I write about the fact that I have cried every morning since Monday, getting in the car and having tears flood my eyes? That I dread Christmas? Do I write about not being able to write since there is so much to write? Does that make any sense at all? What about my desire not to have anything at all to do with Christmas this year? My mind and heart ache for Mom and Pop. I had hoped to turn this journal into a book to help people understand their grief, but I can't imagine being able to help someone else when I am totally unable to help myself.

Mad at God?

In March, Princeton sponsored the annual women's retreat. A guest kept talking about how angry she had been in the wake of certain personal trials and losses. She said that God had revealed to her that she was angry at God. She would not let that go. I don't think I am angry at God. Is it possible that I am and don't know it? If I am not angry at God, why did this woman's repetition of the theme bother me so much? I kept hearing, probably more often than she said it, "mad at God." Mad at God, mad at God, mad at God resounded like a drum beat in my head.

November 23, today, I went up to the cemetery. For the first time I admitted out loud that I am angry at God. Why did He take Pop and Mom? Why did He take them both at the same time? And why did He have to allow them to be so disfigured by the fire that I could not see them again? I am angry. **I love God and I know He loves me. I am still angry though, and He knows that.**

This is a December journal note. Oh God, I love you. I trust you. I am trying to trust you. I just don't see how any of this pain fits in with your plan. Maybe, if I could see that there was a purpose for this pain, it would make it all worthwhile. Is there some way you plan to redeem this hurt? Please, please don't leave me here sobbing and ignorant. Give me a hint as to your divine plan. Please. Please...

New Year's Eve, I needed to tell God that I don't understand His plan. I feel so alone, so broken. I do not understand why He would let me fail so badly on Christmas Eve. I am angry. I am hurt. I might as well tell Him, since He already knows. I don't understand how the God who loves me would take Mom and Pop away from me. I still need them. I pleaded with God to show me His will for me, His plan or even a hint of it. I need to know whether He even wants me to be in ministry anymore.

In April, over a year after the accident, I was still angry. Juanita asked if I was angry at my parents for leaving me without my consent. That is not it. My father was a good driver. He almost regained control of the car. Had it not been for the location of that concrete culvert, he would have recovered that control. They would have had nothing more than a thrilling, scary story to tell. I am not angry at Pop. Accidents are sometimes unavoidable. Actually, I am not even angry anymore that Mom and Pop have died. I was prepared for that to happen someday. I am angry that they died so horribly. God could have prevented the horror of the fire. He could have made it possible for me to see my parents again at peace and neither in pain nor afraid. God could have prevented the fire damage to my parents' bodies, but He chose not to do so. **I am angry!** I have no idea what to do about it. All I can do is tell God about my anger and ask Him to help me release it.

Social Media

I have come to see Facebook as a tool to journal my grief. I have a group of friends who are willing to read and pray with me about both the good days and the terrible days. The following posts illustrate something of my online journal on Facebook. They are landmarks in the fog.

April 26. I am declaring a Yay me day. When I got home from church, I got a reluctant lawn mower started, and I mowed the yard today. I never had to do it before. This is one more step in the process of becoming an independent person and property owner, one who is responsible for all, not merely a couple, of the household maintenance chores.

May 22. I just wish I could thank them. Not through their words only but through the lives they led, my parents taught me about the importance of family, about unconditional love, and about faith in Christ. They taught me to pursue my dreams. They provided a foundation on which to build a life. They provided all the necessary tools to become the person I am. If only they had taught me how to be without them. I guess that's for me to figure out.

September 2. If you are not in the frame of mind for a little testifying... feel free to scroll on by. This afternoon on the way home, a phrase from 1 Thessalonians 5:16-18 (NIV) came to mind, "Be joyful always; pray continually; give thanks in all circumstances, for this is God's will for you in Christ Jesus." You know, it is really easy to give thanks when everything is going the way we want it to go. Doesn't mean we always give thanks then, but then it is easy. "Give thanks in all circumstances," means ALL circumstances. I realized that this also meant in an accident that took my parents six months ago. All circumstances even includes the accident. So, this evening, in the car, I had a little praise session. I thanked God that Mom and Pop did not have to watch each other fade away as so many lifelong loves do. I thanked God that Mom no longer has to worry about her ability to serve her beloved Plum Creek Church. I thanked God for the love that let them go home together and for the loving, praying friends who have surrounded me. Giving thanks in all things frees us to enjoy the good and trust in God through the bad. I felt so good to be able to offer this praise, even for the accident. In ALL circumstances, God is good, or to use a familiar phrase, "God is good all the time!"

Facebook may not be your thing. It is important to find some outlet, some place where you can pour out your heart. Tell your stories. Share your memories. These things will bring healing to your broken heart. You may also bless those who remember your loved ones fondly.

New Normal?!

If you have dearly loved the one who has died, if they were a daily part of your life, their presence was part of your normal world. You may find yourself picking up the phone just to say hi. In your old normal, you could do that any time you liked. You may go shopping and find a special treat for the one who is gone. In old normal, you did things like that for one another. Now, there is no one on the other end of the line, no one whose face will light up at the sight of the special treat. The ways you find to accept and adapt to these absences are part of your new normal.

I have engaged in a long period of figuring who I am now that I can no longer define myself as being Beth and Willis' daughter. It takes a long time to move from "we" to "I," and "our" to "my." I still catch myself saying, "We do this or that." I usually apologize and correct myself, "this is something **I** like to do." **This is the beginning of my new normal.**

January 15, 2016. On Tuesday, I got quite a bit done in the office. Plum Creek has encouraged me to join the Osawatomie Ministerial Association. This group met at the Nazarene Church Tuesday night. They called for volunteers to offer the invocation at City Council on Thursday night. I agreed to do that.

On Thursday, I got caught up in the office for the first time since Mom and Pop died. I have had my head in the game all week. I have felt good. I have been able to write some words of comfort for people on the grief sites I frequent. I read four books. I listened to a cd Jane made for me for Christmas. I don't know yet whether this is a brief reprieve or real healing, but for now, it feels good. When I got home from the office tonight, there was a box in the door. It was the t-shirts for Dorothy and me that were not supposed to arrive until next week. I was so excited to be able to take one to Dorothy tomorrow at breakfast. This has been an incredibly good week, productive. I have felt pretty good. Yet, tonight…I do not hurt. I am not crying. I feel empty, tired, and sad; so let down from the highs of this week. I just want to sit here and hug my Pammie. I miss Pop. I miss Mom.

January 16, 2016. I met Dorothy at Plum Creek for breakfast this morning. She was excited to receive her t-shirt. I told her that I had had a pretty good week, gotten caught up, felt good most of the week. I got excited last night about getting the shirts. I was also drained, empty, and totally exhausted. Dorothy said that was a sign that I was getting back to normal. **If I am completely honest, I am not sure that I am ready to be whatever passes for normal in this new life.**

Uncomfortable Condolences

People generally mean well. When they have no idea how to console us, they recommend that we engage in the things that bring them comfort. A Facebook friend wants me to get a puppy. I travel so much that it would be unfair to a pet. And I don't want to have to clean up after one.

I have tried always to respond with grace no matter how vile or horrible the comments people have made. I have not always been successful, but I have tried. I have read articles on what not to say to grieving, hurting people. In the last eight months, I have heard most of them. I am learning what not to say as a pastor! I cannot count the number of times I have heard that I am lucky that I do not have to worry about Mom and Pop going to a nursing home. When I miss them so desperately, these words, even if true, do not help.

Depending on when you read this, you may already be aware that people will say some of the most unhelpful things as you experience your loss. Most people mean well and want to help and bring comfort. They have no idea what to say. It reminds me that in the Book of Job (2:11-13 NIV), Job's friends are good comforters...for the first seven days. For the first week, Job's friends simply sit with him, letting him know that he is not alone. Then for some all too human reason, they feel compelled to speak. And their support is all downhill from there. So, my hope for you is that your friends are first week friends and that they will not feel the need to advise and speak. It took ten months after the accident before I could reflect on some of the themes my comforters offered.

In December, I pondered, "Do I have any insight or wisdom to offer someone else who is hurting? I cannot imagine right now what it would be. I could offer all of the same clichés and platitudes I have been offered. Not one of them is helpful."

"Be strong," is not helpful when one is simply trying to survive. You are trying to survive at a time when you are not even sure you want to survive the heartache.

"They are not struggling with health issues or pain anymore," is true but not at all helpful. Right now I am, perhaps selfishly, more interested in the fact that my heart is broken than that they are now well.

"You are handling this so well." It shows that the speaker has NO idea of what I am going through, how I really feel. If they only knew, they would know that I am not handling this loss well at all. They would see through this thin veneer.

"There is no time limit," or its companion, "Everyone grieves differently," is not especially helpful. They are true but not helpful. I need to know when I will be able to function again. I need answers, not the answer that there are no answers. I sometimes want to say, "Lie to me. Give me a timetable even if you are making it up out of whole cloth. I just need answers." In fact, I made just such a request of Juanita one day. With a gentle smile she said, "Dear one, I don't lie. There is no time table."

Don't ask me how I am doing unless you actually care about the answer. Realize that I can usually tell whether you are asking because you are supposed to or if you care. If you are asking to be polite, you will get, "I'm fine." And you will not pursue it, because if I actually opened up to you, it might make you sad.

As much as I have said about comforters who did not comfort, there were so many more who did such amazingly thoughtful things. Some brought food that was ready to set on the table. They knew I was in no shape to try to figure out what or even how to cook. Some of those food bringers also brought paper goods, disposable plates, napkins and utensils. No dishwashing! For my green friends reading this, I think a time of loss is a legitimate exception to the no disposable dishware philosophy!

One friend understood that we would be mailing out a lot of thank you notes. She sent me a book of stamps. How thoughtful!

Jane brought a Route 44 tea to the visitation.

I received notes with people's memories of my parents. Someone who worked with Pop fifteen years ago came to say Pop had been a nice guy.

People generally mean well. It is not that important to have some brilliant word of hope. Just showing up for someone who is hurting is a tremendous gift.

Laughter

When you can laugh, it may be the most healing activity you can do. When you find yourself laughing again, you will know that life will again be worth living. A few months after the accident, Jane texted me a joke. "What do you call a fly with no wings?.....A walk!" She then warned me never to tell that joke to her again,... but I did!

A friend loaned me a book from our church library. It is called *Laugh your way to grace; reclaiming the spiritual power of humor.* This book meant a lot to me. I consider myself to be a storyteller. The author is a stand-up comedian. We are both pastors. She is a former trial lawyer, and I have an Elder Law practice.

I love to laugh. I do not cry well. Studies show that laughter releases the same healing chemicals in our brains that tears do. So, in the absence of sobbing, howl at the moon, racking tears, I listen to comedians, remember family stories and laugh. I especially like Christian comics like Jeff Allen and Chonda Pierce. For laughter, I also treat myself to the music of Ray Stevens. I love songs like "The Mississippi Squirrel Revival," "Kiss a Pig," and "The Pirate Song." At income tax time, I recommend, "Juanita and the kids." I know it may be too soon for you to find it funny, but I also love Ray Stevens' "Sittin' up with the dead."

I also use humor to deflect attention when someone is getting too close to an issue I don't want to face. Juanita has caught me numerous times throwing out a quip or a one-liner to dodge an uncomfortable question. It never works with her, though. She sees these deflections as red flags indicating something we need to talk further about. She's good!

As I was revising this manuscript, I was interrupted twice one day by phone calls claiming to be from the federal government. Here is what I posted on Facebook, "I am a loyal American, and my government appreciates that. At least I think that is what the two heavily accented voices wanted to tell me in the last two hours. The government appreciates my loyalty and my lack of a felony record so much that they want to give me a grant of $7,000. I don't even have to pay it back. And all they need to complete the grant is my banking information. Isn't that wonderful?! How should I spend the money? Unicorn rides or ocean front property in Arizona?" Sometimes, you have to laugh.

I have so many funny memories, family memories. Every time I laugh, I celebrate those with whom that memory was created.

Mom and I would have pun wars. Maybe Shakespeare did say that puns were the lowest form of humor, but he sure used a lot of them. Mom and I figured if they were good enough for Shakespeare... well. Mom and I could hold entire conversations using nothing but lines from the movies we both loved.

If you need to laugh, laugh. If you need to cry, cry. If they come together, it is absolutely okay.

In D Ark

On February 19, 2016, I was dreading the one year anniversary of the deaths of my parents. I had been posting loving stories and tributes to them each evening on my Facebook page since late January. One friend came to call them my "Bedtime Stories." I knew that when it hit me that they had been gone one full year, it would hit hard. On the 19th, I got home from the office, and I was settling in for the evening as darkness fell. The lights in the house flickered then went out. I waited for a couple of minutes, hoping it was just a temporary outage at dusk. I called to report the outage. It was widespread. I sat in the dark for a little while, feeling sorry for myself.

Why, I wondered, on the anniversary of the darkest week of my life, would God let the electricity go off? Why would He literally leave me sitting in the dark? I have had at least one light on in the house twenty four hours a day for the last year. I could not stand to have the house completely dark. My phone was fully charged, so I posted on Facebook, "Where was Noah when the lights went out? In d ark." A friend thought that was my sermon title for the next week. I had to explain that it was an actual status update, because I was without electricity. I was already beginning to see a certain metaphor, dark night of the soul…dark night of the no electricity.

As I sat in the darkness, I felt, rather than heard God say, "I am tired of having you be afraid of the dark. We are going to sit here together in the darkness until you realize that I am with you in darkness. I am with you when you leave every light in the house burning. I am with you in joy. I am with you in your deep sorrow. And we are going to sit here until you get that." I am a slow learner, I guess. The lights did not come back on for over two hours!

Afterword

On that trip home several years ago, it seemed as though the fog might never end. Dorothy and I made it safely home though. The sun came up the next morning on a beautiful day. Life continued.

The fog of grief also seemingly never ends. Along the way, we may doubt that we will ever see beauty again or ever again hear the sound of our own laughter. Truly, grief never does end, but it does have significantly lighter patches. Life does take on new meaning, and it does become good again. Take courage.

Sixteen months after the accident, I am happy. I love my family, friends, and church. These are the people who travel the foggy way with me. I have found joy and comfort in writing this book.

If I have anything to offer you, it is the assurance that there is hope. There is tomorrow. Prayerful friends and a loving God will carry you. You are not alone even in those moments when it feels most that you are. Life does go on. And life will be good again.

I must be honest with you. Why stop now, right? I have three trusted friends to whom I gave copies of this manuscript for review. I wanted to see whether I was saying too much or too little about some of the events of the year. As I worked on the book, I was able freely to express my doubts and fears, hopes and dreams. They were safe, because they were mine. I was the only one looking at them. No one else could judge them to be valid or invalid. I was safe with them and in expressing them, and they were safe with me. The minute I turned that manuscript over to someone else, I became vulnerable. My private thoughts and fears were exposed. Those ideas were out there. Someone could choose to accept or reject them. They could appreciate my journey or scoff that it had taken me so long to recover. My ideas were no longer merely mine, and they were no longer safe. I had these deep fearful feelings when the people receiving the manuscript were people that I trust. How much worse will it be when anyone in the world can read and opine on my life? I was feeling so vulnerable that I contemplated collecting those copies back and tossing the project. I was afraid. I do not like to be afraid. In that context I read Jesus' words, in John 14:27 (NIV), "Peace I leave with you; my peace I give you. I do not give to you as the world gives. Do not let your hearts be troubled and do not be afraid." I have a story that I needed to tell you. I have a hope in God that I needed to share with you. This book is an avenue for me to do that. Do not be afraid. I had to read that passage twice! Do not be afraid!

May God grant you peace and healing on your journey through the fog. You are not alone. Thank you for reading my story and making it a part of your own.

Light in the Fog

These are some of the songs that comforted me as I made my way through the fog. Most were recommended by good friends.

"Clean"	Natalie Grant
"Deer's Cry"	Lisa Kelly
"May it be"	Lisa Kelly
"If we're honest"	Francesca Battistelli
"Just Be Held"	Casting Crowns
"Set me Free"	Casting Crowns
"Losing"	10th Avenue North
"What you want"	10th Avenue North
"Worn"	10th Avenue North

As a lifelong Johnny Cash fan, I must mention the Man in Black.
"Hurt"
"The Reverend Mr. Black"
"Hidden Shame"
"The one on the right is on the left"

A friend of mine shared a couple of poems that have become very meaningful to me.
"Fresh Grief" by Annette Billings
"Call when you get home" by Annette Billings

Books I have read on grief, adult orphans, and healing:

Levy, Alexander. *The Orphaned Adult; Understanding and Coping with Grief and Change after the Death of Our Parents.* Cambridge, MA.: Da Capo Press, 1999.

Lewis, C.S. *A Grief Observed.* N.Y.: Harper Collins, 1961.

Nouwen, Henri, J.M. *The Wounded Healer: Ministry in Contemporary Society.* N.Y.: Image Books, 1979.

Secunda, Victoria. *Losing your parents finding yourself, the Defining Turning Point of Adult Life.* N.Y.: Hyperion, 2000.

Sparks, Susan. *Laugh your way to Grace; reclaiming the spiritual power of humor.* Woodstock, VT.: Skylight Paths Publishing, 2010.

Westberg, Granger E. *Good Grief.* Minneapolis, MN.: Fortress Press, 1971.

Wolfelt, Alan D., PhD. *Healing The Adult Child's Grieving Heart, 100 Practical Ideas after your Parent Dies.* Fort Collins, CO.: Companion Press, 2002.

Wolfelt, Alan D., PhD. *Understanding Your Grief; Ten Essential Touchstones For Finding Hope and Healing Your Heart.* Fort Collins, CO.: Companion Press, 2003.

I have found these Facebook sites and groups to be helpful:

The Empty Chair
Encouragement for those who have lost a father (Closed group)
Encouragement for those who have lost a loved one
Encouragement for those who have lost a loved one due to a traumatic event (Closed group)
Encouragement for those who have lost a mother (Closed group)
Grief Speaks Out
Grief Toolbox
Healing Hugs

CPSIA information can be obtained
at www.ICGtesting.com
Printed in the USA
FSOW02n0111240916
25328FS